BlindSpots

ALSO BY STEVEN S. SIMRING, M.D., AND
SUE KLAVANS SIMRING, D.S.W.

Making Marriage Work for Dummies

The Compatibility Quotient

BlindSpots

Stop Repeating Mistakes That Mess Up Your Love Life, Career, Finances, and Happiness

STEVEN S. SIMRING, M.D.
SUE KLAVANS SIMRING, D.S.W.
AND FLORENCE ISAACS

M. EVANS
Lanham • New York • Boulder • Toronto • Plymouth, UK

M Evans
An imprint of Rowman & Littlefield
4501 Forbes Boulevard, Suite 200
Lanham, Maryland 20706
www.rowman.com

10 Thornbury Road, Plymouth PL6 7PP
United Kingdom

Distributed by
NATIONAL BOOK NETWORK

Library of Congress Cataloging-in Publication Data

Simring, Steven S.
Blindspots : stop repeating mistakes that mess up your love life, career, finances, and happiness / Steven S. Simring, Sue Klavans Simring, and Florence Issacs.
p. cm.
ISBN 978-1-59700-240-9
1. Self-defeating behavior. I. Simring, Sue Klavans. II. Isaacs, Florence. III. Title
BF637.S37S56 2005 158.1—dc22 2005007471

Book design and type formatting by Bernard Schleifer

Manufactured in the United States of America

To Gene Busnar,

whom we will always remember with love

Contents

Acknowledgments

THROUGHOUT OUR CAREERS IN MENTAL HEALTH, WE HAVE BEEN working with patients to help them see their own behavior more clearly. The idea of writing a book on this subject came from a series of meetings that we had with Gene Busnar. Gene was a musician-turned-writer, who helped us refine our ideas and develop the concept of discrete BlindSpots. Halfway through the process, Gene suddenly and tragically died. We are so very indebted to him and to his wonderful wife, Liz, and his daughter, Nadeen.

It is no easy task to pick up someone else's half-finished work, but Florence Isaacs did it masterfully. Florence is a very talented writer. She has been endlessly patient with us, absorbing our ideas and giving them shape and form. We are deeply grateful to her for the magnificent job she has done.

Of course, nothing would have happened without our super agent, Linda Konner. After helping us focus the concept, Linda introduced us to Gene, then to Florence, then to PJ Dempsey at M. Evans and Company. PJ and her firm are throwbacks, in the best sense of the word, to what publishing used to be—involved, helpful, caring, and hands-on.

Steven S. Simring, M.D.
Sue K. Simring, D.S.W.

Introduction

The definition of insanity is doing the same thing over and over and expecting different results

—BENJAMIN FRANKLIN

MOST OF THE PATIENTS WHOM WE SEE AS PSYCHOTHERAPISTS ARE QUITE accomplished people. They are intelligent, good at what they do, and have families and friends. Many earn impressive incomes. They come to see us because certain patterns of behavior keep getting them into trouble.

A forty-two-year-old executive remains stuck at a mid-level management position. Everyone tells him that he does a great job, but whenever he applies for a promotion, he says the wrong thing and gets passed over by a younger colleague.

A middle-aged woman owns a thriving fashion manufacturing business. She has always earned a good income, yet has no savings for retirement. Although she has put a great deal of money aside for this purpose, she's lost it. She has been misled by a series of bad investment advisers.

A twenty-five-year-old man is about to lose his driver's license. He admits to us that he speeds a lot, but he explains that all his friends speed, too. When his friends get pulled over, he says ruefully, they almost always manage to talk their way out of trouble. Not him. He starts arguing with the cop and invariably gets a speeding ticket—along with an extra summons for a broken taillight.

Over the years as we listened to these stories, we began to ask ourselves the question: "Why do smart people make dumb mistakes—and make them over and over again?" The issues that got these individuals into trouble were very obvious to us and to almost everyone else around them. Yet these patients were blind to their own destructive behavior, although they saw everything else quite clearly.

We noticed that other smart people we knew—friends and colleagues—were no different. They made the same mistakes repeatedly, and blamed the outcomes on others or on bad luck. Somehow, they never seemed to see what they were doing wrong. And of course we always knew that we ourselves were not exempt.

We identified a number of specific "BlindSpots"—lapses of vision that tripped up even the smartest people we know. These BlindSpots caused predictable patterns of behavior that regularly ended in grief. If we could only see the dangers, we reasoned, we would know the steps to take to protect ourselves.

Clinical experience convinced us that specific BlindSpots were characteristic of particular individuals. One person would be vulnerable to one type of BlindSpot and not to another. Sometimes a BlindSpot would emerge only in certain situations or areas of a person's life. He or she might have a rewarding career and a disastrous personal life. Success in one area did not guarantee success in others. We also found that people tended to underestimate themselves and their strengths. They had far more power to take positive action than they realized.

There is no inoculation against BlindSpots. They're part of the human condition. But there is an antidote—self-awareness. Patients ask us all the time in therapy, "What don't I understand? What am I doing wrong? What am I missing?"—and we help them find out. We can help you, too. By using some of the same tools we employ in our own practice, you can, in effect, become your own therapist. You can start to recognize your own BlindSpots and become better able to see them coming before it's too late. Techniques that have worked for our patients will help you analyze your missteps, learn from them, and prevent heartache and disappointment. You'll also discover what you're doing right.

Picture your life as a journey down a highway. There are likely to be stretches of open road that are easy to negotiate at a brisk and steady speed. You are also bound to encounter unexpected obstacles and sudden turns that challenge your ability to predict what lies ahead. Sometimes you need to make a quick decision in order to avoid a crash. In other instances, you may not be certain about which route to take or how best to pace yourself. This book will guide you on your way—at home, at work, and in the world. You're going to find yourself saying much less often, "Oh, I did it again!"

Part I

BlindSpot Basics

CHAPTER 1

What Is a BlindSpot?

Freedom is just chaos with better lighting.

—ALAN DEAN FOSTER

A BLINDSPOT IS AN EMOTIONAL OBSTRUCTION SIMILAR TO THE BLIND SPOTS that impair vision on the road and lead to automobile accidents. Imagine yourself driving down the highway. Suddenly you decide to change lanes. You don't see a speeding car in the other lane approaching from the rear. Unless you change course, a collision will take place, but you have a blind spot that makes you unaware of the imminent danger. Emotional BlindSpots also stop you from seeing potential dangers—in life. These BlindSpots fog your vision and trigger self-destructive behavior patterns that lead to foolish decisions. Because you can't see clearly, you make damaging mistakes in relationships, finances, your career, or the rest of your life.

BlindSpots explain why you always jump into love affairs that end badly or stay stuck in dead-end situations. They're the reason why you make ill-advised investments or business decisions over and over again without ever seeming to benefit from past experience. BlindSpots stop you from navigating the inevitable obstacles that turn up in life—and taking corrective action to get around them.

All of us have exercised poor judgment at one time or another, and admitted, "I didn't see that coming." But occasional missteps aren't what we're concerned about here. BlindSpots are different. They're characterized by repetitive, almost compulsive behavior. To qualify as a BlindSpot, your poor judgment must have occurred again and again in the same or similar situations. Maybe your broker calls to give you the same pitch he did the last two times when the stocks he touted were losers. If you proceed to invest in his new pick because you think this time he's going to make money for you—you've got a BlindSpot.

If you repeatedly choose men who are emotionally unavailable or women who are shallow and irresponsible or friends who drain you and ignore your needs, you've got a BlindSpot. If you allow coworkers to take credit for your accomplishments again and again or remain in a miserable job year after year, refusing to look elsewhere, you've got a BlindSpot.

How BlindSpots Operate

When you have a BlindSpot, the reality of a situation is right before your eyes, but you don't see it. You're unable to think rationally. You believe that the next time (or the next person) will be different, despite clear evidence to the contrary. And you're blind to the fact that your method of dealing with the issue (whatever it is) doesn't work. Worse, your pattern of behavior perpetuates the problem. Imagine you're a parent, and your child hangs out with the wrong crowd, regularly breaking curfews. Your solution is to yell and punish him or her. When your child's behavior continues, you react the same way over and over again—with more punishing and more yelling. It's obvious to any bystander that you are stuck. But you can't see that. You are unable to do anything different. You can't stop and say to yourself, "Wait a minute. This isn't working. Maybe I need to try something else." You keep repeating the same ineffective action. Faulty reasoning stops you from problem-solving and finding another, more effective solution.

The same irrational thinking and lack of vision invites deception by others, which is why con men thrive on our BlindSpots. When a salesman offers you something for nothing, or makes extravagant promises that are hard to believe, you push aside the nagging feeling that perhaps something is wrong—and forge ahead.

Whether fooling yourself or being conned, you not only ignore your own doubts, you're deaf to warnings from others. You become engaged to someone who's been married twice before. The person's own mother says you're making a big mistake. But you convince yourself all will be well. You don't want to hear any news that would alter your plan.

Where You Encounter BlindSpots

BlindSpots turn up in any area of your life—your marriage, social life, family life, money matters, your job. They surface when emotions run high. If you feel threatened, afraid, angry, overwhelmed, or excited, you're vulnerable to a BlindSpot because you can't reason properly. When you're madly in love with a business deal (or a new romance) you can't be objective. BlindSpots are common around love and money because people are often irrational in these areas.

BlindSpots also show up when you make major purchases. We almost bought a house years ago that would have been a great mistake. It was a beautiful, wildly modern house by a famous architect that captured our imagination. It had wonderful turrets, gracefully curving walls, and lots of glass, but it was wrong in every other way. We needed enough room to raise a growing family and to live in an area with a good school system, which this town didn't have. Although the house design was gorgeous, the curved walls reduced the amount of living space and there was no air conditioning. The children's bedrooms were in a separate building from the main house.

The only goal the house met was aesthetic, which reminds us of the late designer Philip Johnson's comment when asked to define a comfortable chair. In his view, a comfortable chair is a chair that is good to look at. If your objective is to sit comfortably and read a newspaper, however, that is not the piece of furniture you want to buy.

We almost bought the house despite its drawbacks because we wanted it to work for us. We made rationalizations. "We don't need air conditioning; there aren't that many hot weekends during the summer," we assured ourselves. "So there isn't much space. We can live with round walls, and we don't really need thermopane glass in the windows." Fortunately reason eventually triumphed. It was a great house, but there was no room for the children.

We were seduced by the glamour of the house and the idea that people would walk by and say, "Wow, look at that." BlindSpots are seductive, too, because they're an easy way out. They allow you to ignore the difficult issues you need to face, rather than confront them. They let you put yourself in someone else's hands, rather than do the hard work of making reasoned decisions. BlindSpots soothe you, enabling you to rationalize "I've done what I can" when you actually haven't. If taking the easy out, abdicating power, and rationalization become excuses for missing opportunities and making poor choices, you've got a BlindSpot.

BlindSpots' Range of Impact

BlindSpots develop throughout your life, and we all have them. In fact, we usually have several. BlindSpots can be limited and confined to a particular situation, as when you repeatedly ignore signs that a business deal is no longer in your interests and stubbornly cling to your decision. Or the same BlindSpot and pattern of behavior may arise in different arenas. For example, you don't see that your boss is dissatisfied with your work—and you also don't see that your spouse is unhappy. In some cases a BlindSpot can be pervasive throughout your entire life. If you're an extremely anxious person, your intense emotion stops you from thinking clearly whether you're buying a condo, hiring employees, estimating retirement needs, or starting an extramarital affair.

BlindSpots also vary in intensity. A BlindSpot may be so mild, it causes little or no trouble. For example, you may feel intimidated about speaking up in large groups, but have no difficulty voicing your views in other situations. In your line of work, the BlindSpot doesn't really hurt you. However, more intense BlindSpots can cause real trouble, leading you to act recklessly—or passively allow disaster to strike without taking measures to protect yourself. At the far end of the spectrum, a very severe BlindSpot can ruin your life. It can get you into legal difficulties or even send you to jail. It can wreck your marriage or torpedo your career. The challenge is to take control of your BlindSpots rather than let them control you. That's what this book is all about.

Identifying BlindSpots

Each individual BlindSpot has its own unique characteristics. But there are four general tip-offs that you've got one operating at any given time. You know a BlindSpot may be at work if:

- You're not getting the result you want.
- Something similar has happened to you in the past with a negative outcome.
- People tell you, "You're making the same mistake."
- You ignore a gut feeling, no matter how faint, that tells you something may be wrong.

Overcoming BlindSpots

You need to deal with your damaging BlindSpots because they stop you from reaching your goals, block your success, and undermine your general happiness and well-being. To help you modify or eliminate them, we've developed a five-step prescriptive process that we call the "Foolproof Plan."

The Foolproof Plan will help you achieve the following life-changing benefits:

- Move beyond powerful emotions that distort your judgment.
- Recognize whom to trust—and whom to distrust.
- Know what you really want from people—and what they want from you.
- Understand how the messages you think you're transmitting are being received.
- Make accurate decisions by teasing out facts from blind emotion and using them to your best advantage.
- Defend yourself against other people's BlindSpots.
- Reach goals and get more of what you want in your personal and professional life.

Once these interlocking skills are in place, your ability to predict and control the outcome of events will improve dramatically. You'll achieve this critical leap of awareness with the help of a variety of strategies. The tools we provide are based on years of clinical experience, and field-testing our techniques for effectiveness.

The need to deal with BlindSpots has never been greater. We live in an age of unparalleled uncertainty and skepticism, when it seems more difficult than ever to trust in the good intentions of others—not to mention our own judgment. The ongoing threat of terror and global war has further undermined our collective sense of control and well-being. This growing insecurity has contributed to an environment in which we are increasingly vulnerable to both the lies others tell us and the lies we tell ourselves.

We plan to lead you through the fog of deception into the light. You'll be able to anticipate trouble and minimize or avoid it by saying to yourself, "Stop! I know that I am vulnerable in certain areas. Am I making decisions or taking action for the wrong reasons? Am I thinking clearly and taking responsibility for my own happiness?" Regardless of the answer, you'll be on your way to greater control of your own life.

How to Use This Book

Our goal is to give you the power to accurately size up people, situations, and your own motives with new precision—and expand your possibilities in life. Here's how to use this book to accomplish these aims:

1. Assess how large a role BlindSpots play in your life right now by filling out the Initial BlindSpot Inventory in chapter 2.
2. Learn about the eight critical BlindSpots in chapter 3, and see which ones you identify with (and recognize in others).
3. Read through the Foolproof Plan in chapter 4 to understand how to analyze and deal with BlindSpots in general.
4. To confirm identification of your own personal BlindSpots, take the short quiz at the top of each BlindSpot chapter. Chapters 7 through 14 are devoted to each of the eight critical BlindSpots. They describe the BlindSpot in depth and show you how to overcome it by applying the Foolproof Plan.
5. Read chapter 7, BlindSpot #1 *Wishful Thinking*, first because this BlindSpot works in tandem with many others. Then, if you prefer, read the BlindSpot chapters that most apply to you. But we urge you to read every chapter, regardless of the order you choose. Even if a particular BlindSpot is not a problem for you, you will find useful tips and other information that can help you handle many situations more smoothly. In addition, these chapters will help you recognize BlindSpots in other people. No matter how good a driver you are, you have to anticipate the blindness of others whose actions can put you in jeopardy.
6. Read the concluding Part III of this book (chapters 15 through 19) to recognize the part you play in destructive behavior patterns, and learn how to change these patterns; to deal with other psychological barriers; and to know when you need more than a book, and professional help is required. In-depth success stories illustrate how people have overcome their BlindSpots. The last chapter helps you evaluate your progress and handle adversity as you continue to master your own BlindSpots. You will also learn how to cope with other people's BlindSpots that affect you.

CHAPTER 2

Assess Your BlindSpots

Better a mistake at the beginning than at the end

—African saying

EVERYONE HAS BLINDSPOTS—POLITICIANS AND PILOTS, PHYSICISTS AND college professors, billionaires and the rest of us. You're susceptible regardless of your IQ, your bank balance, your education, or your occupation. To get a reading of the role BlindSpots play in your life right now, fill in the questionnaire below. Your answers will pinpoint areas in which BlindSpots are causing trouble, and start you thinking about ways you tend to deceive yourself.

INITIAL BLINDSPOTS INVENTORY

Instructions: Using a 5-point scale, rate each statement below as follows:

1 = disagree most of the time
2 = disagree some of the time
3 = agree and disagree about equally
4 = agree some of the time
5 = agree most of the time

__ My decisions usually have the outcome I anticipate.

(There is a correspondence between the way you think events will turn out and the way they really do. If you're often scratching your head and wondering "How on earth did I get in this mess?" you've missed seeing relevant factors or information that would have helped you succeed or at least avoid trouble.)

__ When a situation doesn't work out, I can see the gaps in how I sized it up.

(To stop repeating mistakes, you must understand where you went wrong. Just blaming bad luck when things don't work out, stops you from looking any further and examining your own role in a fiasco—such as failure to research a project or deal before you jump in.)

__ I am usually able to avoid being overcome by strong emotions such as love or fear that distort my judgment.

(Everyone has periods of strong emotion, but are you able to see that these are not times to make decisions? Can you step back and recognize, "I'm too angry to think clearly. I'll decide tomorrow, after I calm down.")

__ I am pretty good at recognizing whom to trust—and whom not to trust.

(Do you have a pattern of being abused by others or being disappointed in people? Is your trust well placed in friends, colleagues, or those offering professional help, such as an accountant or a real estate broker? There's a balance between being overly mistrustful and missing out on opportunities.)

__ I understand what I want from people.

(Can you focus on your goals, without being distracted by someone's charisma? If your goal is a sensible investment, it has nothing to do with the personality of the salesman—or the financial consultant's glamorous client list.)

__ I am good at perceiving what other people want from me.

(Do you always feel people take advantage of you? Can you recognize when someone wants to be a friend and when that person simply wants information from you or a combination of both? If not, you're going to be disappointed in others.)

__ The messages I transmit to others are received by others as I intended.

(Are there lots of misunderstandings in your life? Do you think your spouse or employees should be able to read your mind and know what you want without your telling them? Does what you say or do often misfire? If you regularly insult people unintentionally or you never get called back after job interviews, you're sending the wrong messages.)

__ My sense of timing in terms of when (and when not) to act is right on the money.

(Timing is everything. Do you always buy or sell at the wrong time or ask for raises too early or too late? Are you able to bail out of projects when conditions change and the odds of success are no longer in your favor?)

__ I take responsibility for my shortcomings and mistakes, and I expect others to do likewise.

(If you always have an alibi, you can't problem-solve efficiently and improve your performance next time. Offering excuses and lamenting, "Poor me," causes repeated mistakes.)

__ I feel I am in control of my own destiny, though I'm aware that certain things are outside my control.

(Awareness of your limitations is essential in life. Realize that you can't know everything and events can't always work out perfectly. Exaggerating your abilities or underestimating them can crush you, or at a minimum lead to disillusionment. Success lies in finding a balance, setting realistic goals, and knowing what you can accomplish.)

__ TOTAL

If your total score is:

45–50: You have little problem with BlindSpots.

37–44: Relatively minor problems across the board, or notable problems in one or two areas.

30–36: Possibility of serious BlindSpot issues in one or more areas, or moderately serious issues across a somewhat wider spectrum.

25–29: Likelihood of serious BlindSpot issues in three or four key areas, or moderately serious issues in five or more areas.

24 or less: Probability of dangerously serious BlindSpot issues in several key areas. Likelihood of serious deception issues in five or more areas, or moderately serious issues in seven or more areas.

If your score is 45 or over, you are generally self-aware. There probably aren't any major areas of your life where BlindSpots do damage. A score of 37–44 indicates your BlindSpots are causing a little trouble. Pay attention. If your score is 25–36, your BlindSpots are getting serious. Beware of self-destructive behavior. A score of 24 or less suggests you have very serious BlindSpots throughout your life. Be sure to consult the Foolproof Plan in every BlindSpot chapter to illuminate areas where you get into trouble and change what you're doing.

Conditions That Make You More Vulnerable to BlindSpots

Be aware that certain conditions make you more of a target for BlindSpots. Strong emotions or overinvestment in advancing agendas can evoke BlindSpots. Life changes and loss can also trigger BlindSpots. Watch out for trouble under these circumstances:

Intense Emotion

Anytime adrenaline flows—you feel threatened, nervous, afraid, angry, overwhelmed—it raises your level of anxiety and distorts your vision. Very positive emotion, such as feeling passionate about someone or something, also stops you from seeing clearly or thinking rationally. For example, pressure to make a fast decision or get quick results puts you at risk for BlindSpots because stress impairs judgment. If you're under the gun to boost sales (or get married) you're more likely to be open to taking foolish risks or cutting corners.

Change

Change, even good change like taking a new job, getting married, having a baby, or moving to another locale stirs anxiety along with joy and other strong feelings that impair your reasoning powers and make you more vulnerable to missteps. Even a promotion puts you at risk for trouble. Becoming the boss is a role change involving added responsibility, shifts in relationships with coworkers, and other tensions that may cloud judgment. You may also become a target for others to undermine.

Loss

All losses cause emotional vulnerability—getting laid off, financial setbacks, the end of an affair, divorce, death—which in turn triggers BlindSpots. At these times, your self esteem plummets and you're too overwhelmed by grief to make thoughtful decisions. In the months after his wife of twenty years left him, *The New Yorker* movie critic David Denby writes in his book *American Sucker* that he lived years of madness. He became obsessed with online porn and cars, and had an affair with a married woman. He sustained huge losses in the 2001 stock market plunge. Everybody gets a little crazy during the early stages of a separation. Because the trauma of loss reduces your ability to think, it sets you up for deception by yourself or others.

Agendas

If you want to prove something, you're more concerned about your own needs than the facts of the situation and less open to examining the pros and cons of a decision. If you need to prove you're still desirable after your spouse has left, you're likelier to find excuses to get involved with someone who puts you down and takes your money.

Try to remember that these are "red flag" situations when you need to stop and think in order to stay out of trouble.

CHAPTER 3

Identifying the Eight Critical BlindSpots

Repeating mistakes is more likely than profiting from them.

—MALCOLM FORBES

BLINDSPOTS STOP YOU FROM REACHING YOUR FULL POTENTIAL IN LIFE, and our goal is to help you deal with yours. We've identified eight critical BlindSpots—emotional gaps in vision that cause repetitive errors in judgment and unhappy outcomes in relationships, finances, and careers. These eight BlindSpots are:

1. Wishful Thinking

This BlindSpot is the belief that something is so because you *want* it to be so—at work, at home, or in money matters. *Wishful thinking* is the wish that a deal that offers something for nothing is legitimate, or your coworkers will like you, or your future mate will stop gambling after the wedding. You persist in this thinking despite ample evidence to the contrary. For example, maybe you consistently overspend, figuring, "Next year, I'm going to make more money, and I'll be able to handle these payments." Then next year comes and the economy doesn't cooperate. You've got the *Wishful Thinking* BlindSpot.

Wishful thinking ran rampant in the year 2000, when millions of people watched the stock market begin an astonishing nosedive. As prices dropped steadily, investors continued to hold on to their shares. "The market will turn around," they assured themselves, and their losses piled up as they held fast. "After all, how low can stocks go?" they rationalized. Both wealthy and working-class people clung to a strategy that obviously wasn't working. Some lost so much money that they had to shelve their retirement plans. Now they kick themselves for not selling out early. "How could I have sat there and done nothing?" they ask in wonder.

2. Not Knowing When You're In or Out of Control

When you have this BlindSpot, you overestimate or underestimate how much control you have in a given situation. You attempt to "fix" or change your spouse or mold your unathletic child into a sports star—unsuccessfully, and at high cost to the relationship. Or you cling to a relationship going nowhere year after year, convinced that eventually, you can make the person want to marry you. Usually, you're disappointed. You believe you're in charge when, in fact, you are not. This is the BlindSpot that allows you to consistently take on too many projects, overestimating how much you can accomplish. Often you wind up exhausted and unable to meet deadlines. Your reputation suffers.

Conversely, you may feel helpless to act on your own behalf when you really *do* have power. You perceive yourself as lacking options when the opposite is true, or you devalue your own strengths. For example, you have trouble setting limits and saying no to others. In ways large and small, you often wind up doing what you don't want to do. When you have career plans, but your family insists you join their business (or the military) instead, you feel your only choice is to give up your own fulfillment and go along.

3. Believing in Myths

You accept the truth of folklore, myths, or trite sayings and ideas, such as "Happy couples never fight" or "Hard work will always be rewarded"—without examination. You live your life by them—at home, at work, and everywhere else. Because these myths often are based on half-truths or old truths that are no longer valid, believing in them can damage relationships, careers, and much more.

For example, you stay in a job waiting and waiting for a promotion you deserve but aren't getting—instead of sending your resume around and looking elsewhere. This BlindSpot stops you from protecting your own interests and achieving your objectives. It also supports wishful thinking, providing excuses to avoid necessary change. Family myths are particularly destructive.

4. Not Knowing How You Come Across

You misperceive how others see you. This BlindSpot sinks careers and personal relationships (and causes politicians to lose elections). Because your view of yourself is distorted, you can't see the reactions you provoke in others and don't realize how angry, arrogant, or insensitive you appear. The converse is also true. You may present as funny, articulate, and smart, and be oblivious to your appealing presentation. When you don't know how you come across, you also overlook or misinterpret the context of interactions and misjudge what people want from you. You may be blind to people's agendas and forget to watch your back. For example, when you go out on job interviews, you neglect to do your homework on the company or prepare yourself to discuss the strengths you can offer to fill its needs. Instead, you focus on what *you* want out of the job. Then you wonder why you aren't called back.

5. Looking for a Hero

You become so dazzled by another person, especially in the areas of money and romance, that your judgment is impaired. You idolize and ascribe "magical powers" to the individual—and put yourself in his or her hands to make money for you or protect you or confer special status. However, you do this with little evidence that your trust is well-placed. Then you wind up disappointed, or in serious financial or personal trouble. This BlindSpot puts you at risk when you need expert advice of any kind.

You're drawn to charismatic lawyers or financial advisors or celebrity doctors without considering whether they really meet your needs.

6. Being a Hero or Savior

This is the flip side of *looking for a hero*. When you have this BlindSpot, you regularly rescue other people—in order to meet your own needs as much or more than theirs. You like being placed on a pedestal, or you feel that you aren't valuable unless you are helping someone else. You're attracted to needy people, including love interests who are always in trouble financially, legally, or emotionally.

For example, you marry one woman after another who is depressed or spends all your money. Or you're always bailing people out of jail or trying to get them jobs. Your "good deeds" drain you because these people frequently don't want to help themselves—and they stop you from getting involved in more meaningful, positive activities and balanced relationships.

7. Overwhelming Emotion

Strong feelings of love, fear, jealousy, rage, grief, sadness impair your judgment. You rush into impulsive, destructive decisions and leap to reckless action as a way to deal with the cascade of feelings. Often you burn your bridges without considering the downside. For example, after a client causes you trouble, you insist on venting your rage and writing him an irate letter detailing his transgressions. You make an enemy. A year later, he moves to another company you're pitching and is in a position to block you from winning the account. This BlindSpot leads you to make impulsive or irrational decisions in relationships, finances, and other areas of your life.

8. Bad Timing

You miss opportunities (or otherwise hurt yourself) by acting too early, too late, or not at all. You lack vision. You fear taking prudent risks and pass up good jobs. Or you fire someone hastily, without considering the consequences for everyone else's workload. Or you stall marketing a product; by the time it comes out, it's already out of vogue. This BlindSpot affects relationships, too. Perhaps you split with your spouse before giving reconciliation a real chance. Later, you regret rushing into divorce. But by this time, your ex is happily remarried. You feel the relationship could have been saved if you hadn't left so soon and been unwilling to work harder on problems.

Identifying and Changing BlindSpots

Do you recognize yourself in any of these BlindSpots? Which ones? Different people have different BlindSpots, and some BlindSpots are easier to see than others, depending on how self-aware you are and the situation in which it is operating. How easy or difficult it is to change a BlindSpot depends on how severe it is. BlindSpots that are deeply ingrained in our personalities are the hardest to modify because personality usually doesn't change. For example, if you come across as too aggressive or angry, and those qualities are entrenched in your personality, you're going to have a more difficult time changing your BlindSpot than someone who is only aggressive or angry under certain circumstances or when dealing with particular situations or individuals.

Gender Differences

BlindSpots are no more common in one gender than the other, but the way BlindSpots manifest themselves sometimes differ for men and women. As clichéd as it sounds (and although there's a big overlap), men and women *are* socialized differently in our society and therefore experience the world differently. For example, men are generally less likely to go to the doctor than women are because they're expected to be independent rather than ask for help. They may blindly ignore physical signs of serious medical problems and convince themselves they're really fine when they are not. As a result, men are more apt to get into trouble regarding their health when they have the *Not Knowing When You're In or Out of Control* BlindSpot than women are. On the other hand, women are more likely to nag when they have that BlindSpot. They feel helpless to get what they want and think (erroneously) that nagging will produce results.

Men often are unaware of the effect of their yelling on others. They don't realize that their physiologically louder and stronger voices intimidate women and children. This gets them into trouble at home when they have the *Not Knowing How You Come Across* BlindSpot.

Women who have the *Believing in Myths* BlindSpot, are more likely to have trouble speaking up for themselves and taking credit for their accomplishments at work. They've been socialized to believe they should be modest.

Moving Toward Solutions

Now that you've been introduced to the eight critical BlindSpots, you're going to learn how to start acting in a more effective and focused manner. When you have BlindSpots, you behave in ways that are contrary to your own self interest. You have an uncanny ability to ignore both the facts and the wisdom of past experience in key life areas. We're about to show you how to live smarter—and a lot happier.

CHAPTER 4

The Five-Step Foolproof Plan

Fool me once, shame on you; fool me twice, shame on me.

—CHINESE PROVERB

Mistakes are a natural and important part of life and often beneficial. However, we can help you open your eyes, learn from experience, and stop making the same errors of judgment over and over again. Even the brightest among us may have trouble benefiting from missteps. When we chronically land in the same predicaments, we sometimes see ourselves as victims of some cosmic system of destiny that we are powerless to change. "Why me?" we ask.

We've developed a program that we call the Foolproof Plan that helps you break the vicious cycle and start acting more effectively. When you've got a BlindSpot, you want something (such as a better social life) but repeatedly take actions that produce the opposite results—you alienate people. Or you sit by passively or procrastinate and prevent good things from happening. Instead of going to social events, you stay home and deprive yourself of the chance to make new friends. The Foolproof Plan works on two fronts to effect change by:

- Helping you stop behaving self-destructively before damage is done, and while there's still time to change course and get what you want, or

- Helping you analyze past mistakes instead of justifying them, see what you could have done differently, and understand why you didn't see the truth earlier.

You can lead yourself through these steps for any BlindSpot and in any situation where you're not getting the expected result—or when someone is telling you, "You're doing it again." The steps force you to be brutally honest with yourself and face the gap between what you want and what you need to do to achieve it.

The Five-Step Foolproof Plan

Step 1. Focus on your objective.
Step 2. Separate fact from fantasy.
Step 3. Recognize and remove emotional roadblocks.
Step 4. Ask for feedback to inspire positive change.
Step 5. Act in your best interests.

Step 1. Focus on your objective.

The first step of the Foolproof Plan is to know your goal. Keep your eye on it whether it involves buying a house, getting hired, launching a new relationship, or investing for retirement. When you have a BlindSpot, you lose sight of your objective. There's a disconnect between the goal and the steps you take to reach it. You get distracted or sidetracked and follow a course of action that doesn't get you where you want to go. Ask yourself periodically, "Am I achieving my objective?" If the answer is no, you need to change your strategy or plan.

If your goal is to get married, but you're nowhere close, what is your strategy? If you're in a relationship with someone who's always traveling on business and won't commit, you're not moving toward your goal. What you're doing isn't working. You need to think about changing course. Perhaps it's time to leave and pursue other options.

Or maybe you're a college teacher whose goal is tenure. The unspoken rule for tenure is do a lot of research and publish in journals.

If your strategy is to rely on your superior teaching skills and popularity with students instead because you hate research and writing, you're likely to find that plan won't get you where you want to go.

Perhaps you're an artist whose goal is to develop repeat business. You meet a collector who likes your work and buys one of your paintings. She tells you to stay in touch. If your strategy is to call her every week to chitchat, you risk cooling her interest. There's a line between staying in touch and being a pest. You want to develop a business relationship with your client. She isn't one of your friends.

Such mistakes happen all the time. Lack of objectivity and failure to set or stick to a goal lie at the heart of many disasters. Sometimes you also need to *clarify* your goal. If your objective is to find a job that allows for a large amount of family time, you need to look for a position that doesn't require long hours and accept that you won't necessarily get rich. If you interview at large firms, you probably aren't going to achieve your goal. You might make lots of money but you also might have to work many nights and weekends. If you're not clear about the limits your seventy-hours-a-week schedule will place on your family time, you're kidding yourself.

If you want to get married, what kind of marriage do you want? What are your values? How important is religion? Do you want to go to church every week? Or not. How important is a family-oriented life? If so, what does that mean to you? Can you work late—or do you expect to eat dinner together every night? Do you have to attend *every* family event? Do the kids go *everywhere* with you? How important is a large amount of leisure time to pursue sports or hobbies or cultural interests? Is leisure time more important to you than a high income and affluent lifestyle? Do you genuinely enjoy your work or is it just a way to make a living?

Often your vision is an abstraction and your goal is poorly defined. It's essential to establish well-defined goals. When you do this you have a far greater chance of achieving your objective and making choices that will further your vision. On the other hand, as you refine your goals, you may find that your vision is unrealistic. It might have to change.

Step 2. Separate fact from fantasy.

After you focus on your objective, the second step in the Foolproof Plan is to separate fact (reality) from fiction (your own version of the facts). Your version may suit your purposes or spring from lack of confidence. Like a good detective or investigative reporter, it's important to keep your focus on "just the facts," rather than on what you would like the facts to be or mistakenly think they are. When you do, you are less likely to fool yourself or be deceived by others.

The task is to read the facts correctly and make choices based on that reading, not on the "sizzle"—the glamour of the situation or the charisma or magnetic personality of the salesperson. To acquire the tools to detect the truth, use due diligence and look for clues.

Exercise due diligence, which is the hard work of checking out the facts, the people involved, and the opportunities and pitfalls in a situation. For example, real estate agents often show you a house on Sunday. You're impressed with the quiet little street. But unless you come back at various times on weekdays, you won't see that the charming street is a major commuter thoroughfare. Very few of us do this kind of research.

If you've got an idea that you think has great commercial potential, it's natural to want to move ahead and implement it. But first you have to make sure the product really works, the market is really there, and that investors will back you. One key element in checking out facts is to look at the track record. Then you'd discover that the ski resort you want to buy into may have great trails, but it hasn't turned a profit in years.

Due diligence is an art. It is not fun; it's time consuming and it's boring. Which is one of the reasons we don't do it. It's easier just to barrel ahead. Some of us wind up with a string of failures because we won't do the research necessary to protect ourselves.

Look for clues when you're searching for the truth. If you meet a salesman or a colleague for the first time and walk away saying "John Jones is a fantastic person. I think he's impressive, and I really trust him," you'd better be aware that you've just been seduced. Too much charm is always a danger signal. Trusting relationships develop slowly over time, not in one meeting. There's a difference between reacting positively to a person and making a real connection—and feeling drugged, a state where good judgment is suspended. If you're madly in love after the first date, watch out. You're a prime target for a BlindSpot.

If a person is secretive and evades your questions, beware. Don't ignore a nagging doubt in your gut that something doesn't add up. Pay attention.

Step 3. Recognize and remove emotional roadblocks.

The third step in the Foolproof Plan is to recognize factors that stop you from thinking rationally. Getting the salient facts helps you deal with BlindSpots, but the facts won't help you much if you can't process and use them. Here are some factors that limit your ability to reason:

Anxiety. Anxiety can be so powerful that it distorts your vision. You can't accurately recognize danger or interpret information that is right before your eyes. You see nonexistent safe harbors, or bogus risks that stop you from taking action. Fear of change and risk and the anxiety that goes along with it runs through many BlindSpots.

For example, maybe you were an architect who refused to face the fact that computers were taking over your business years ago. "They're just a fad. They'll never last," you told yourself. You felt anxious and threatened by the need to learn a totally new way to work. "What if I can't pull it off? What if I fail?" you asked. Because you couldn't adapt, you gradually lost business you counted on. Commissions stopped coming in, and you went out of business.

Denial. This particular concept of denial isn't saying the facts are not true—it's denial of what the facts mean. This concept of denial is easily seen in alcoholics. Alcoholics don't say, "I don't drink." Instead they insist, "I drink, but it's no big deal. I can handle it." They recognize the facts but see them through rose-colored glasses. All BlindSpots involve denial.

Depression. Depression, which distorts your perception, is the most common emotional problem in our society. You often don't know you're depressed. The outlook seems bleak, when that is not the reality. As a result, you may pass up opportunities because you view minor problems as hopeless.

Stubbornness. This stops you from considering new information that might cause you to take another direction or change your strategy. You stick with one plan or decision, regardless of its merits, to the exclusion of all others. Resolve is a positive attribute when combined with good sense, but it transforms into mere rigidity when judgment is missing or impaired.

Impulsiveness. This drives you toward immediate action, while blocking out any and all facts that would deter or slow you down. If you're overly impulsive, you look for a quick fix, and accept a terrible settlement when breaking up your business partnership just to get it over with fast. Or you plunge ahead into dubious projects or relationships. Acting too hastily increases your vulnerability to all sorts of trouble.

Desperation. Desperation narrows your focus and limits your thinking, and therefore your possibilities. It makes you an easy target for deception because you feel overwhelmed and will often grasp at any straw. You're so focused on your pain that you shut out information that could help you out of the dilemma. For example, if you're forty-two years old, divorced, and desperate to prove you're not a failure at relationships, you might shut out evidence that your new love does drugs.

Step 4. Ask for feedback to inspire positive change.

Without facts, you can't deal with a BlindSpot—and feedback is a major way to get facts. The right kind of feedback illuminates BlindSpots. It provides information you might not have considered before, clarifies thinking, and enables you to reevaluate the situation you're in. Only then can you begin to make changes.

Turn to others for information and advice to help you make decisions and deal with a tough problem, whether it's office politics, conflict with your spouse, or trouble with your kids. Sometimes relatives and friends can provide the information you need. At other times, you may have to find outside professional help, such as an accountant, attorney, school guidance counselor, or therapist. For career-related issues, network and rely on others' assistance. For example, one way to distinguish an industry fad from a permanent change that requires you to make adjustments is to consult with colleagues and learn from their experiences.

Also pay attention to feedback you receive without asking for it, especially when others warn you to stay away from a person or company or business deal. As one of our family members used to say, "When everyone tells you you're dead, lie down."

Step 5: Act in your best interests.

Watch out for distractions from your goal. Imagine negotiating for a new home and telling the real estate broker your bid—only to hear this response: "You're insulting the seller. I won't even bring such an offer to her." This is a fairly common scenario, and you may either withdraw the bid or feel so intimidated that you raise the offer considerably. But you're the buyer, and your best interests have nothing to do with pleasing the seller or burnishing your own image to avoid looking like a cheapskate. These issues aren't relevant. You don't even know the seller. This is just a business transaction. The goal is to obtain a house you like at a price you want to pay and can afford. If you can't accomplish that, you have to let the house go. Wanting to be liked or appearing "nice" are not appropriate motivations here.

Understand who's responsible for past fiascos. If you've lost money to con men more than once, get to the bottom of why. Were you fooled by an irresistible sales pitch or by your own glaring

BlindSpot that made you a ripe target? It's often easy to confuse the two, but you have to take responsibility for your own vulnerability to deception.

Those who set out to fool others have done their homework. These operators are usually masters of applied psychology. They have a keen understanding of the people they target and their vulnerabilities. Whatever the context or potential stakes, it's always perilous to let yourself be taken in—whether it's through deception that's initiated by you or by someone else. Doing so can lead you to make bad personal, financial, and career choices that can have serious long-term consequences.

Manage competing desires. To determine your best interests when you have competing desires, sort out which of your choices has *the most meaning at this time.* Maybe you've been laid off, when suddenly you receive two different job offers. One will boost your career, almost double your previous paycheck, and provide the security of working for a rock-solid corporation. But the hours are nine to five—and you have two preschool children. The second job with a promising start-up company pays substantially less. The company's long-range future is not guaranteed. However, you can telecommute and only have to go in to the office one day a week.

You want the money, opportunity, and safety offered by the first job. You also want to raise your children. How do you choose? Tease out what is most important to you *at this point in your life.* That's difficult because you then have to let go of other benefits you want. If the deciding factor is money and career opportunities, you join the first employer. If above all, you want flexibility while the children are young, you choose the start-up.

Realize that the answer today may change later. After the children reach grade school, you could revisit the idea of a nine-to-five job at a higher salary.

Taking Control of Your Future

The five-step Foolproof Plan arms you with the tools to understand your mistakes and avoid repeating them. We'll show you how to apply the Foolproof Plan to your own BlindSpots in chapters 7 through 13 ahead. As you learn how to overcome your BlindSpots, you'll gain a fuller knowledge of yourself, other people, and the quickly changing world around you.

CHAPTER 5

How Major Life Changes Affect BlindSpots

A fault confessed is half redressed.

—PROVERB

YOU GET MARRIED . . . YOU RETIRE . . . YOUR KIDS REACH THE TEEN years . . . all of us face transitions over the course of our lives. And everybody is especially vulnerable to BlindSpots at these turning points when there are exits and entries into our lives or shifts in status. It's simply that BlindSpots tend to emerge at times of major change. Change, even good change, shakes your equilibrium. It raises your level of anxiety and distorts your vision of what's really going on. Change creates fertile ground for self-deception and deception by others.

New behaviors are often required to negotiate transitions in the life cycle. Because emotions tend to run high at these times, BlindSpots can impede healthy adjustments. Nobody escapes without a certain amount of turmoil, but knowing what to expect helps you navigate turning points more smoothly and prepares you to deal with trouble.

BlindSpots intensify built-in pressures and tensions at each stage of life. You are particularly at risk for BlindSpots when negotiating the following life tasks:

Finding a mate. During this time, you're vulnerable to choosing a partner for the wrong reasons. You may select an inappropriate or incompatible mate due to parental pressure or because you feel out of sync with your friends. They're all married or involved in serious relationships, and you feel compelled to find a partner, too. You may want a relationship so badly that you don't see problems. You blind yourself to warning signs that someone is immature, unreliable, emotionally unavailable, dishonest, or an otherwise unsuitable match. Declining fertility puts extra pressure on women over thirty-five who want to have a family.

Another common reason for choosing an inappropriate mate is difficulty in being alone. Both men and women struggle with loneliness. Regardless of gender, you may feel you have no value unless you attach yourself to someone else. You may never have learned how to feel good about yourself when you are on your own—or how to build a community of friends you can turn to for companionship and intimacy. The desperate need to be connected increases the chances that a BlindSpot such as *Wishful Thinking* or *Overwhelming Emotion* will emerge, causing you to ignore glaring differences in values or other incompatibilities or faults in a potential partner. The same need to be attached may keep you in a relationship that is going nowhere. You convince yourself that the person will eventually commit when it's clear to everyone else that will never happen.

Getting married. A wedding is a joyous occasion, yet full of BlindSpot pitfalls. First, it's common to feel scared to death now that you've made a commitment to another person—and fights about wedding arrangements and the color of the furniture during the period between the engagement and the marriage often mask that fear. This is actually a good time to see if your doubts about the other person have any basis in reality. Yet you may not want to accept facts that might upset your marriage decision. The possibility of a change of heart may be too threatening even to contemplate, leading you to brush off obvious evidence that you are making a mistake. The emotionally charged atmosphere can also affect practical matters. You may neglect to sign a prenuptial agreement when that is a wise thing to do.

After the wedding, you may think that marriage is going to solve preexisting conflicts like how much time your wife talks on the phone with her mother or how much time your husband spends with friends. Disagreements may only be premarital jitters and quickly dissipate, but sometimes they reflect genuine differences you may have been blind to in the first blush of love, such as where you are going to live or how you are going to arrange your work schedules.

The reality is, life gets more complicated after you've formalized your commitment. Even if you've previously lived together, roles and responsibilities have to be negotiated. Rules and attitudes about issues like money, friends, and vacations change. Every couple must build its own family unit, setting new boundaries with families of origin and dealing with loyalty shifts. Your primary loyalty is now to your new wife or husband, yet you want to maintain a strong connection to your parents and siblings. It's a balancing act. All of these changes set the stage for BlindSpots such as *Wishful Thinking* and *Not Knowing When You're In or Out of Control* to increase tensions.

Birth of a child. More divorces take place after the first child arrives than at any other point in a marriage. You probably have unrealistic expectations of how your life and your roles will unfold after the birth, triggering BlindSpots such as *Believing in Myths.* You believe that going from two to three is easy to do. But life after baby doesn't remotely resemble life before—and this causes a great deal of conflict.

You're usually unprepared for the radical changes in your couple relationship after a child arrives. The two of you and your needs are no longer the focus of the household; the infant is. Unless you come from a large family, you probably have no experience with the enormous demands of child care and the division of labor that occurs. Paternity leave is still not a reality for most men, and fathers may become jealous of the intense mother-child bond that seems to exclude them. Or if you're a woman who had planned to continue working, you may find to your shock that you really want to stay home to care for your infant.

A baby also severely restricts your freedom as a couple to come and go and the amount of time you spend together. A husband recalls, "When our first child was born I thought I'd never have sex again." That wasn't all. He and his wife could no longer go out to dinner or see a movie together without careful preparation. All of these issues create emotional and economic tensions that must be discussed and dealt with to adjust as a couple and stay close.

Parenting a teenager. It's not easy to parent an adolescent. Teens test limits and are exposed to more (and different) dangers than younger children, such as automobile accidents, alcohol, drugs, and sexual risk taking. You have to allow teens more freedom and make other changes in the way you parent while also providing appropriate supervision to be effective at this time. But the *Not Knowing When You're In or Out of Control* BlindSpot may get in the way. Or you may use *Wishful Thinking* to assure yourself your child isn't touching drugs or engaging in sex when the opposite is true. "Not my child," is a common reaction.

It is also common to think that you can rescue teenagers from difficult situations, such as legal trouble or fights with friends. The question to ask yourself is, "Am I providing appropriate support or filling my own need to *be a savior*?" Is there a BlindSpot at work here?

Reaching middle age. BlindSpots like *Overwhelming Emotion* and *Bad Timing* lead to many of the divorces we see in people in their forties and fifties. Maybe the mirror tells you that you're losing your hair, and you know your knees can't take you skiing anymore. At the same time, you're being passed over for promotions at work for younger people. You feel restless and unfulfilled, and you blame your condition on your wife. It's her nagging and lack of appreciation that is causing your unhappiness. Yet the underlying reason for your discontent is your own aging, which is too hard to acknowledge. Your overwhelming fear of getting older stops you from coming to terms with your waning powers. Instead of dealing with your fear of aging, you have an affair.

Or you feel unfulfilled as you approach menopause. You think this is your last chance to find happiness because you still have your looks and can attract men. This is a time when wives may launch affairs and leave their marriages. He's the wrong husband, you decide, instead of facing what's really happening to your own self-image. You're terrified of aging and becoming less attractive.

The empty nest syndrome brings dissatisfaction and spouse-blaming, as well. If you stayed home to care for the children, you may be more vulnerable to the loss of your daily mom role than career women because you've lost a full-time job. You may also be blind to your husband's discontent at this time. Marital disintegration can come on like a freight train, and you wind up in therapy saying, "I can't believe it. He walked out on me." The BlindSpots are *Bad Timing* and *Wishful Thinking*—believing that a marriage that existed primarily for the welfare of the children will hold together the same way it did before.

You may not anticipate trouble, even when you have very little going for you except common parenting, and it's predictable that when the children leave the house, you're going to have problems. Or you may realize that you're in trouble, but underestimate how bad it really is. *Wishful Thinking* leads you to believe that it will be just as easy for you and your spouse to relate after the children are gone as it was when they were around to act as distractions and a buffer between you.

BlindSpots about health are another serious issue in middle age. You might have been able to ignore the effects of overeating, smoking, and lack of exercise at age thirty, but at fifty-five, the risks of cancer, heart disease, and other life-threatening conditions grow immediate. *Bad Timing* and *Not Knowing When You're In or Out of Control* can be fatal.

Getting divorced. Divorce is devastating to both partners. Feelings of guilt and failture are often strong. The split involves overwhelming emotional, as well as financial, losses. Friendships change as people gravitate to either you or your spouse, or drop you altogether, but rarely stay connected to both of you. A woman may feel she's lost status when she's no longer "Mrs. Somebody." If you've been left, the disappointment and negative impact on self-esteem, trust, and sense of well-being can weaken your reasoning power and even your health, leaving you ripe for deception. BlindSpots like *Looking for a Hero* are one reason divorcing spouses are counseled not to date right away. You are too susceptible to unfortunate romances on the rebound.

Parenting a married child. When your son or daughter gets married, you must adjust to a new relationship with your child. You'll need to get used to a different kind of closeness than what you've been accustomed to. The *Bad Timing* BlindSpot may surface, blinding you to the reality that your child's prime responsibility is now to his or her spouse, not you. You may have unrealistic expectations at this time, failing to recognize that boundaries must change—and that your child must accommodate in-laws and integrate routines and rituals of the spouse's family.

Surviving a spouse or parent. The *Overwhelming Emotion* BlindSpot commonly follow major losses. Your mate's death impacts on every aspect of your life in ways you'd never dreamed. You lose a friend, a lover, the couple lifestyle, and possibly financial security.

Although the death of an older parent is an expected part of the life cycle, it's usually a shock nonetheless. Your mother or father is gone forever, along with your own identity as a son or daughter. You've suddenly become the older generation.

In either case, you may unrealistically expect to be back to normal six weeks or six months after the funeral, underestimating the grieving process and the time it takes to restore a reasonable sense of equilibrium. You walk and talk, and your friends think you look okay, but you don't see how debilitated you actually are. Because grief interferes with the ability to reason, recent widows, widowers, and other bereaved people are at high risk for being taken advantage of by con artists.

Retiring. Retirement causes another radical transformation of roles that invites the *Not Knowing When You're In or Out of Control* BlindSpot to surface. Disconnection from the workforce may cause a decline in self-esteem if you're a man or woman whose identity was wrapped up in your job. The change is usually less of a jolt for a woman because women are more accustomed to having multiple roles. The radical adjustment for women usually involves changes in the marital relationship. Suddenly your spouse is home full time and wants you to have lunch with him, when you have your own work or other interests.

Finances are another stress as you age. As a senior, you have less control over your economic future than in your younger days. Increased medical costs and shrinking pensions can cause financial problems. Whether married or single, you are also in the age group most vulnerable to being taken advantage of by others, like telemarketers. You were brought up to be polite to people, and you're not comfortable hanging up.

Coping with Transitions

Life-cycle changes are treacherous because you're going to have BlindSpots during transitions—everybody does. If you believe you're seeing clearly at these times, that in itself is a BlindSpot. Transitions take a toll on reason.

Overwhelming Emotion, almost by definition, is a factor in every transition. But each phase of life also lends itself to certain other BlindSpots, especially if you already have a tendency toward them. We don't know why you're susceptible to one BlindSpot and not another, although your phase of life and your personality play a role.

Be aware of how your present stage of life increases your own vulnerability to BlindSpots. When you anticipate and prepare for potential problems, you give yourself extra protection against painful mistakes.

CHAPTER 6

Tools for Making Better Life Decisions

If you don't make mistakes, you don't make anything.

—PROVERB

WE'VE DEVELOPED SOME ASSESSMENT TOOLS TO HELP YOU MAKE better decisions when you face problems associated with BlindSpots. We will refer you to these tools at certain times in the chapters ahead. In the meantime, get a head start and become familiar with them. As you learn more about each individual BlindSpot, you'll be able to use these assessments to head off errors of judgment, understand past mistakes, and make good choices in the future.

The Relationship Truth Detector

This 20-question assessment tool can be applied to any potential partner before entering into a major commitment. It can also be used to evaluate a current partner, or applied to an old relationship to see how and where it went wrong. It gives you the opportunity to assess three different kinds of clues:

Section A

External cues about a person. These can be gathered by asking the opinion of others, or noting the comments they offer on their own. Trusted friends and family members who know and love you can be decent judges of future success, especially if most of them agree. Be careful not to block out negative feedback because you want to be in love, or feel desperate, or don't like hearing any information that might cause you to alter a decision you've already made.

Section B

Cues from the person's behavior. From body language to verbal cues, people show their true colors. Some traits are apparent at a first meeting. Other traits form consistent patterns over time. Love is one of the most blinding of all emotions, so it's often easier to catch negative behavioral signs early—before passion overwhelms your better judgment. If you notice a pattern that troubles you, pay close attention to it. Discuss your concerns with the person, or with someone whose feedback you trust. If you remain uncomfortable, proceed with extreme caution, or not at all.

Section C

Internal messages. These are judgments you make on the basis of your own assessments. In order to become foolproof, you need to be your own best judge—as well as your own best friend. Many judgments are based on gut feelings or relatively few facts, so you need to notice your reactions and be courageous in your evaluations.

Relationship Truth Detector

Instructions: On a 5-point scale, rate each statement below as follows:

1 = disagree most of the time
2 = disagree some of the time
3 = agree and disagree about equally
4 = agree some of the time
5 = agree most of the time

Section A

__ 1. My friends think he/she is a good partner for me.
__ 2. My family thinks he/she is a good partner for me.
__ 3. I feel proud to have him/her accompany me to business and social events.
__ 4. I have information that suggests that he/she has been honest about his past or current life.
__ 5. I am free of outside pressures that might weigh heavily on my decision to make a commitment.

Section B

__ 6. He/she is generous, but not excessive, in the handling of money.
__ 7. He/she is dependable and considerate to me and to others.
__ 8. When he/she is angry or upset, he/she manages his/her emotions without attacking me or other people.
__ 9. He/she appears to be unencumbered by substance abuse or other serious destructive habits.
__ 10. He/she is open and honest in sharing feelings, and otherwise trustworthy.
__ 11. He/she challenges me to keep growing as a person.
__ 12. He/she is a good listener.

Section C

__ 13. We agree on most of life's basic values and respect each other in areas where we differ.

__ 14. We have talked about our personal histories and the emotional baggage each of us brings to the relationship. Should problems arise in the future, we would both be willing to seek professional help.

__ 15. If I have a setback, become ill, or do not age gracefully, I feel confident that his/her love for me will not waver.

__ 16. I feel completely safe and secure with him/her emotionally, physically, and sexually.

__ 17. Should we have children, I feel he/she would be a good parent.

__ 18. I am able to live with him/her—despite any flaws and quirks.

__ 19. Should he/she have setbacks in his/her career or his/her health, I am willing to use whatever resources I have to help and support him/her.

__ 20. We are best friends, able to deal with any problems or obstacles that may present themselves.

__ Total

If your total score is:

90 or more:	This is a really good person for you.
75–89:	He/she has lots of good qualities but there are some problems to address.
60–74:	There are about as many pluses as minuses—in terms of hanging in or moving on.
59 or less:	This person doesn't meet your long-term goals, even though you may feel attracted to him/her.

Risk Assessment Inventory

Use the Risk Assessment Inventory to evaluate the pros and cons of taking a risk in any area of your personal, professional, or financial life. To take inventory, divide a sheet of paper into two columns and list the dangers of the step you want to take in one column and the benefits in the other. It sounds simple, but writing down and seeing the advantages and drawbacks makes them concrete and helps you separate realistic concerns from unrealistic ones. For example, perhaps you want to leave your job to go back to school to study for a new career. The columns below clarify the dangers and benefits of making this change.

Dangers	Benefits
Loss of income	Increased future income
Additional expense of tuition	Doing what I enjoy
Possibility of flunking out	Boost in self-esteem
Flooded job market at graduation	Wide choice of specialties
Less time for spouse and children	Prestige and perks of professional career

Past Performance Inventory

One way to function optimally in life is to play to your strengths. But BlindSpots may limit your ability to appreciate your accomplishments and lead you to stress negatives instead. You may dwell on your shortcomings without understanding what your strengths really are. When you know what you're good at, you can focus on those areas—and avoid activities for which you are unsuited and likely to turn in a poor performance.

To sharpen your vision, take an inventory of your biggest successes (situations that you handled very well) and your worst flops (situations that you managed badly) in recent years. The sample job-related inventory below indicates some possibilities to illustrate what you should be looking for.

HANDLED WELL	HANDLED POORLY
1. Getting new business	1. Negotiating a raise
2. Leading projects	2. Taking orders
3. Chairing committees	3. Being a committee member
4. Training personnel	4. Servicing clients
5. Finding better job	5. Hiring people
6. Networking	6. Fundraising

Take a sheet of paper and compose your own inventory for your social life or any other area of your life. What does the inventory reveal about your strengths and weaknesses? The objective is to use the information to find a good match for your skills whenever possible, and engage in doing more of those kinds of activities at which you excel. You just naturally feel good when you perform at your best level.

Source Evaluation Questionnaire

When seeking feedback it is crucial to approach the right people. You need to know who is trustworthy and who has appropriate information. This questionnaire clarifies what you should be looking for. It helps you answer the question "*Is This Feedback Source Appropriate?*"

RELATIONSHIP TRUTH DETECTOR

Instructions: Circle Yes or No for each of the questions below:

1.	This person knows me well.	Yes	No
2.	This person is very knowledgeable about the problem area.	Yes	No

3. This person has a track record of being trustworthy.	Yes	No
4. This person is not overly emotionally involved in the issue or situation.	Yes	No
5. This person is unlikely to be too biased about the situation.	Yes	No

Analyzing Your Responses

Following are considerations for each of the questions in the assessment tool.

1. Someone who understands your strengths and weaknesses is usually more helpful than someone who is overly impressed with you.

2. Look for the experts. You need to assemble your own think tank, depending on the situation. If you're trying to land a corporate job, members of your professional organization, a placement consultant, or a career coach are all possibilities for valuable information. To place your parent in assisted living, a social worker, elder-care attorney, and friends who have already negotiated the process can help.

Be open to unconventional feedback, as well. For example, sometimes even a competitor may be useful if the person is not directly vying with you in the particular situation. Your best source of information on how to succeed next time may be the enemy himself. Perhaps it's commonly known that a certain professor is the main opponent to your tenure application. He effectively blocked you from reaching your goal. Your first response may be to avoid him, which is the worst possible thing to do. How can you develop arguments to counter his point of view unless you find out why he opposed you?

Try approaching him. Look him in the eye, and say, "I know you've been trying to block me and you're powerful. What can I do to change your mind about my tenure?' That strategy might be a very effective move. Maybe your research was headed in the wrong direction. He might suggest improvements you need to make, such as modifying it to become more compatible with what others in the department are doing. There's a chance you can win him over as an ally. In any case, you'll be no worse off for trying.

3. Be aware that there are people who may envy your success, affluence, or even your child's good grades. Watch out for so-called helpers who undermine your marriage, take your money, mislead you, or tempt you into amoral or corrupt activities. It's important to jettison such negative friends.

4. No one is totally objective, but some people are less emotionally invested in a situation than others. Beware of someone who has a special agenda. If you want feedback about marital problems, you probably shouldn't be talking to a friend who is bitter about divorce. Also beware of people who dispense advice they are unqualified to give. They don't know what they don't know.

5. Someone who is not emotionally involved in a situation may yet have a rigid view of it. The person may be biased and unaware of the bias. If you want feedback about whether you should have a vasectomy, don't ask someone who opposes birth control.

Part II

Overcoming the Eight Critical BlindSpots

CHAPTER 7

BlindSpot #1: Wishful Thinking

Wishing, of all employments, is the worst.

—EDWARD YOUNG

TO FIND OUT IF YOU HAVE A *Wishful Thinking* BLINDSPOT RATE EACH statement below as follows:

1 = disagree most of the time
2 = disagree some of the time
3 = agree and disagree about equally
4 = agree some of the time
5 = agree most of the time

__ I convince myself that situations at work or elsewhere in my life are going well, when it turns out the opposite is true.
__ When I really want to do something, I talk myself into it even if it isn't a wise move.
__ I think other people want the same things I want.
__ I often take risks in my personal life, financially, or in my career that wind up hurting me.
__ Once I've decided on a course of action, I resist changing it regardless of new information that comes to light.
__ TOTAL

Your score and what it means:

20-25: *Wishful Thinking* is a major problem.

15-19: You have some serious deception issues.

8-14: A few issues need attention.

7 or less: You have little or no problem with *Wishful Thinking*.

Any score above 7 means you're someone who believes what you want to believe, regardless of the reality.

Understanding This BlindSpot

The first emotional BlindSpot is *Wishful Thinking*—believing that something is so because you want it to be so. *Wishful Thinking* happens all the time, which is why it's so easy to get into debt, lose money on investments, choose the wrong mates—or even buy clothes that don't fit you. You long for what you don't have: riches, success, acceptance, love, a more exciting lifestyle. And you decide how the story will end. This BlindSpot is particularly common in romantic situations, where thinking with your heart rather than your head gets you into trouble. *Wishful Thinking* keeps you picking the same wrong kinds of people. You rationalize away their chronic irresponsibility, infidelity, or inability to commit because you want the person to be the man or woman of your dreams. Then you pretend the relationship is proceeding in the right direction—that you're going to marry your soul mate and live happily ever after because that's the ending you want.

With this BlindSpot you don't question what you're doing because you don't want unpleasant facts to get in your way. Imagine you're lonely and looking for a serious relationship. When the new man/woman you met gets drunk on your first date, *Wishful Thinking* stops you from asking yourself, "Hey, do I really want to see this person again? Could this be a sign of an alcohol problem?" When you are guilty of *Wishful Thinking*, you don't want to see evidence that might lead to doubt and deter you from your course. You want what you want when you want it, and there is no examination of whether the pursuit of your wish makes sense or of what the consequences may be.

This BlindSpot also affects decision making around money and finances. For example, the two-seater sports car you want to buy won't hold all the equipment you need to tote around, but *Wishful Thinking* convinces you it will work fine. You ignore or make excuses for unwelcome facts that argue against choosing that car. Last year, you talked yourself into a vacation place in Tahiti, rationalizing away any doubts about how often you could get there. *Wishful Thinking* can mislead you about any major purchase because you're seduced by "the sizzle" and ignore what makes sense for your needs.

Wishful Thinking also causes procrastination, passivity, or avoidance of conflict or hassles. These behaviors keep you stuck in a safe, comfortable place instead of acting to protect yourself or achieving something more meaningful in your life. When it's clear to everyone else in the firm that you'll never be made a partner, *Wishful Thinking* keeps you waiting for recognition, instead of exploring opportunities elsewhere. This is also the BlindSpot that encourages you to take your marriage for granted rather than conduct checks on how the relationship is going. You may paper over disagreements rather than discuss them or ignore your mate's expressions of discontent, telling yourself, "Nothing serious is wrong."

It's not uncommon for people who ignore obvious warning signs to see the light after the damage has been done. But by then it's often too late. *Wishful Thinking* ends when your spouse walks out, your boss fires you, your long-neglected house burns down, or you're diagnosed with cancer after smoking for thirty years. At that point, you can't help but see the truth, because it's slapping you in the face.

The Dangers of This BlindSpot

Wishful Thinking is dangerous because it leads you into legal or financial trouble, damages relationships or careers, and even threatens your health. It prevents you from seeing the whole picture at first glance or looking further to expand your view. It allows you to rationalize so you can continue to do what you want to do. Extreme examples are corporate officers who cook the books and shady politicians who accept illegal favors. "How did they think they could get away with it?" we wonder.

Wishful Thinking scripts include: "My husband rarely comes home at night, but he's very happy with our marriage." When he finally leaves, you're shocked. It's dangerous to ignore signs of trouble in your relationship because it stops you from discussing problems with your mate and problem solving. Or the self-talk may run, "I've been feeling chest pains, but it's probably nothing. I don't need to call the doctor or go to the emergency room." That's dangerous—you could have a heart attack.

Wishful Thinking is an easy way out (at first), which is why it's the BlindSpot we see most often. The question is, how far will you attempt to travel on the flimsy wings of your fantasies? At some point, reality is going to catch up with you.

What's Behind This BlindSpot

Wishful Thinking is extremely powerful, which is why this BlindSpot can be so insidious. What's behind it is false hope. Hope is a wonderful and necessary thing in circumstances such as a potentially fatal illness when maintaining hope can play a vital role in recovery. But the mechanism involved in *Wishful Thinking* is a refusal to consider that the facts do mean what they appear to mean. When hope becomes a substitute for sensible action, it will ruin you. Hope is positive only *after* you've done everything possible to assure a desirable outcome.

Because reality challenges your thinking, the *Wishful Thinking* BlindSpot also triggers denial. It allows you to deny the meaning of the facts—and refuse to face up to unpleasant reality.

For example, you pull out of a parking space and scrape the car next to you. Instead of leaving a note, you drive away. You don't want to have to deal with the other driver or notify your insurance company and maybe incur a raise in rates. You assure yourself, "I didn't really do much harm. Probably nothing happened." The next day you may get a call from the owner of the car who saw you leave and wrote down your license plate number (or was told about it by a concerned bystander). Then you are cited not only for causing the damage, but also for leaving the scene. Even if you get away with it, you may pay the price of feeling guilty. It's the refusal to face unpleasant reality that gets you into trouble.

Three Key Elements

The behaviors below support *Wishful Thinking.* They make this BlindSpot an obstructive force in life because they fool you into shielding yourself from disagreeable facts with:

Self-Centered Reasoning

Self-centered reasoning has you relying on your own reservoir of knowledge and your own opinions and point-of-view—even when the information is limited and distorted. You continue to reason in a vacuum rather than seek more objective external sources to tease out the facts of a situation. It's a sign you're blind to another perspective if the situation creates more emotional stress than you think is appropriate, or other people tell you you're stuck or you feel that you're stuck.

For example, your seventeen-year-old son has been a disinterested student for years. Now that it's time to apply to colleges, he waits until the last minute to complete applications, needs prodding to get teacher recommendations, and doesn't show up for appointments with the guidance counselor. It's obvious he isn't ready for college and doesn't want to go. But you don't see it because you want him to earn a college degree. You look no further. You assume your son wants what you want and never ask the guidance counselor or other parents for their opinions or advice.

Self-Serving Perceptions

You credit yourself with successes and blame outside forces and other people for your failures. The thinking goes, "I lost money on that real-estate venture because the market dropped," when the real reason was you didn't do your homework and wound up choosing a poor location. It's not your fault you can't ever get ahead with your credit card bills. "The minimum payments are so low—only $25 a month," you insist, as you continue to make purchases and interest piles up. This distortion of information stops you from learning from your mistakes—because you think you haven't made any. Self-protective stories can be effortlessly internalized. You can come to believe them and accept them as the whole truth.

Resistance to Change

This is a natural reaction to fear of the unknown and creates anxiety and doubt. Rather than tolerate this discomfort, it's easier to stick with the status quo. That's part of the reason why we stay in unhappy relationships or remain in a job where advancement is impossible. People have different abilities to tolerate change.

It's easy to become attached to long-established patterns, even when they lead us down treacherous paths. Maybe globalization has changed your business. Industry friends urge you to adapt and offer a different kind of service now in demand—one for which you are eminently suited. Instead you cling to the status quo because it's what you've always done and you're afraid to try something new. Your friends' predictions come true. Accounts dry up and your company fails. We are often ingenious in the ways we use our aversion to change to shield ourselves from unpleasant facts. Yet "the devil you know" isn't always better than the one you don't know. Resistance to change stands in the way of seeing possibilities and shifting strategy. In *Wishful Thinking,* we assume the only right choice is the one we've already made.

Overcoming *Wishful Thinking*

Regardless of where *Wishful Thinking* occurs in your life, you can prevent it from causing havoc again by leading yourself through the five steps of the Foolproof Plan. This process helps you understand why you couldn't see the truth earlier or how your blindness led to poor decision making. The Foolproof Plan also works *during* episodes of *Wishful Thinking* to help you stop what you're doing, think clearly, and change course before disaster strikes.

Step 1. *Focus on your objective.*

Know your goal. Whether your objective is a relationship, a job, or a vacation home, don't lose sight of it. If you're not achieving your goal, you've lost focus or the situation has changed. In either case, you need to reassess your strategy. Don't be afraid to reevaluate. Force yourself, if necessary.

If the goal is to meet someone and get married—and it's not happening—maybe it's because your strategy is wrong and you have to try something else, such as signing up for volunteer work, a sailing club, or other activities where you can connect with new people. If you're working sixteen hours a day, you're fooling yourself that you really want a serious relationship. Change your priorities and get out of the office. Remember, *Wishful Thinking* results from a denial of reality. Because that denial may feel good, it needs to be examined.

On the other hand, if it's unlikely that you're going to accomplish your objective, you may have to let it go or modify it. Helping your child get a college education is a worthy long-range objective. But if your teenager isn't mature enough for college at this time, the goal may have to be postponed.

The point is: It's very hard at first to blow the whistle and say to yourself, "Halt. I'm not sure things are right. Am I distorting information to stop myself from looking at other options?" But you must do it. With practice, it becomes a habit.

Step 2. *Separate fact from fiction:*

Make choices based on real facts and information (not just your version of them). For example:

> *Your version is:* I want to buy a cool sports car.
> *The fact is:* The trunk is too small, you're a salesman who makes calls with large sample cases, and this will be your only car.
>
> *Your version is:* I'm falling in love with someone who tells me how smart and wonderful I am.
> *The fact is:* This person is chronically in debt, unfaithful, or drinks too much.

To avoid getting burned again, take the Relationship Truth Detector test on pages 57–58. This helps you slow down and look closer at someone you're thinking of getting involved with before passion overtakes your judgment—and also assesses your current partner.

Step 3. *Recognize and remove emotional roadblocks.*

Watch where you're going. The path to your goal may be bumpy and strewn with diversions. Beware of self-centered reasoning, self-serving perceptions, and resistance to change. Also look out for:

Panic. This manifests itself in terror that you will lose a once-in-a-lifetime opportunity and incur irreversible damage if you deviate from your plan. You will never get a partnership or a share of the profits. You will never get married. Calm yourself down so you can think rationally and deal constructively with the problem. Try approaches such as meditation or relaxation exercises. Or if necessary, talk to your doctor about medication. You can't be flooded with emotions when you make a decision because you won't reason properly.

Threatened self-esteem or identity. When you are invested in a certain outcome, there's a tendency to deny reality and resist change. If you're educated yourself, you may expect your kids to go to college. If your son wants to become a mechanic instead, you think altering your college plan means admitting you're a failure or incompetent.

That's hard to face. But it's a distorted interpretation of what has happened. It's the plan that has failed, not you.

Step 4. *Ask for feedback to inspire positive change.*

Seek second or third opinions. Explore your perceptions and talk to people who can see more clearly, or at least differently, than you can. Depending on the kind of help you need, a clergyman, guidance counselor, therapist, accountant, or trusted friend or relative can point out the flaws in your thinking. If you've tried to resolve issues with your spouse or someone important to you without success, you may be a candidate for therapy. (See chapter 17.)

Be prepared for bad news. Regardless of who you consult, realize that you may hear what you don't want to hear or have to change your opinion. Remember, ignoring bad news doesn't make it go away. Problems that are not addressed usually escalate.

Look for the "buts." When someone points out, "This is not working (or not in your best interests). You have to try something else," and you reply, "Yes, but . . ." you are rationalizing bad news. Stop finding excuses to justify continuing the same destructive behavior.

Expect uncertainty. If you decide to switch to another plan, realize you may have to endure a period of anxiety and doubt. This happens because once you admit that your present approach isn't working, you disturb the equilibrium and enter a transitional state where you feel uncomfortable. It's important at this time to tolerate the discomfort that always accompanies change and stop repeating the same old behavior. Then you can jettison the destructive strategies that have plagued you.

Step 5. *Act in your best interests.*

Take risks. Risks are part of life. You take a chance when you start a new friendship, get married, change careers, or buy a house. Learn to trust yourself to assess the dangers and benefits of a decision and be able to make a smart move.

Think. If the issue is whether to leave your job, ask yourself, "Is this position serving my purpose?" If the job pays very well and the main goal of the job is to make money, that fact might override any other considerations, such as opportunities for advancement. You also may be better off staying where you are if you need more experience or nobody is hiring in your field. At the same time, you may be hurting yourself if you don't take the new job.

Take a Risk Assessment Inventory. There are risks in anything. Factor in your own gut feelings. If you want to marry, you have to risk getting closer to someone. This inventory helps you compare the real dangers to the benefits of any decision or change. (See page 59.)

A Classic Case of *Wishful Thinking*

Wishful Thinking plays out in a number of ways and in a variety of situations and areas of life. Just one classic case of *wishful thinking* involved twenty-nine-year-old Eileen. Eileen, who was heir to a successful printing business, allowed herself to be deceived and paid for it dearly. She lived with her parents in an insulated upper-class suburban community. Her fiancé, Elliott, was thirty-eight years old, a New York garment-center hustler and womanizer with a taste for cocaine. Elliott was tall, dark, and handsome. He drove a Rolls Royce and maintained a beachfront house. Elliott wanted to be married, but he also wanted his wife to be rich so that he could get out of debt and continue to support a lifestyle that was far beyond his means.

Eileen and Elliott met one August weekend at a trendy nightspot. The couple dated for just two months before getting engaged. She was swept off her feet. Many of Eileen's friends and relatives took one look at this match and predicted certain disaster. By sheer coincidence, a friend of Eileen's cousin had been engaged to Elliott two years earlier, but broke off the relationship when she discovered he was simultaneously engaged to yet another woman. The cousin felt she had no choice but to warn Eileen about what she was letting herself in for. "You're just jealous," Eileen snapped, after her cousin told her about Elliott's double engagement.

Eileen's mother was even more seduced than Eileen was. "The man is definitely a little wild," she told her daughter. "But I'm sure he'll settle down once you're married. A catch like this comes along once in a lifetime, especially for a woman who's pushing thirty. You'd be a fool not to grab this chance."

The 500-guest, black-tie wedding (paid for by Eileen's parents) was an extraordinary study in self-deception. It was as though the event was taking place in two different worlds. Eileen was radiant. But Elliott had invited a large number of friends and business associates to the black-tie affair, many of whom openly smoked marijuana and snorted cocaine throughout the evening. Elliott seemed especially affectionate to one young woman, who actually appeared to be his date. Eileen's friends and cousins watched these proceedings in disbelief.

Less than nine months after the wedding, Eileen filed for divorce. Elliott had never made a secret of his womanizing and drug use, but Eileen (spurred on by her mother's assurances) believed he would stop those activities once they were married. After a few weeks, she realized that she was wrong. Eileen soon moved back to her parents' home, feeling disgraced and distraught.

Eileen might have avoided a great deal of pain if she had accurately interpreted all the warning flares in the weeks leading up to the wedding. Eileen was also privy to specific information (provided by her cousin) that she could have checked out by simply making a phone call.

Eileen wanted Elliott to be the man of her dreams, so she fooled herself and made him so. At twenty-nine, she worried that time was running out for her to find a husband who met her (and her mother's) mythic qualifications. She felt that she was "under the gun," which made it that much harder for her to assess the situation objectively.

The facts were, her fiancé was a manipulative man who needed money, used illegal drugs, and had a clear history of deceiving women. She chose to shut out all internal and external feedback that might have altered her decision to marry him. As so often happens, Eileen's self-deception was exacerbated by many outside factors, including her own anxiety and Elliot's charm.

If Eileen had assessed the facts of her relationship with Elliot with the Relationship Truth Detector (see pages 57–58) she might never have married him. This tool is particularly useful in the process of deciding on the future (or evaluating the demise) of an intimate relationship.

As Eileen started to understand the events that led her to this crisis point in her life, she was able to begin articulating what she wanted in a relationship. Two years after she started dating, Eileen met and married a thirty-six-year-old physical therapist. They're very happy and compatible, although the relationship doesn't have the same kind of magic she felt with Elliott. "Considering my history, that's probably a good thing," she admits.

You've Made a Start

The *Wishful Thinking* BlindSpot costs you money, relationships, success, and peace of mind. It often works in combination with one or more of the other BlindSpots, which you will learn about next. Whether it operates alone or not, however, *Wishful Thinking* can be managed. You can break out of this damaging pattern, gain a clearer view of reality, and accomplish more of your goals.

CHAPTER 8

BlindSpot #2: Not Knowing When You're In or Out of Control

Hope is a waking dream.

—Aristotle

To find out if you have the *Not Knowing When You're In or Out of Control* BlindSpot, rate each statement below as follows:

1 = disagree most of the time
2 = disagree some of the time
3 = agree and disagree about equally
4 = agree some of the time
5 = agree most of the time

__ I try to mold others into the people I want them to be.

__ I ruminate over situations I cannot change.

__ I am overconfident in social, professional, and other situations—or underestimate my own power.

__ After delegating a task to someone, I offer advice or criticize the way it is handled.

__ I have difficulty saying no when I don't want to do something.

__ Total

Your score and what it means:

20–25: *Not Knowing When You're In or Out of Control* is a major problem.

15–19: You have some serious control issues.

8–14: A few issues need attention.

7 or less: You have little or no problem with *Not Knowing When You're In or Out of Control.*

Any score above 7 means that you over- or underestimate your control.

Understanding This BlindSpot

The second emotional BlindSpot is *Not Knowing When You're In or Out of Control*—misperceiving what you can and cannot control in your life. This BlindSpot could explain why you're miserable in your career, why you never get the help you need, or why you think you can change your mate or child—despite ample evidence to the contrary.

Of course you want to control what happens to you, but this BlindSpot leads to one of two miscalculations about power and control:

You overestimate how much power you have in a given situation, and take reckless risks or set yourself up for disappointment. For example, you marry believing that you have the power to "fix" your spouse in very fundamental ways to become the person you want him or her to be. You think you can turn a workaholic into someone who takes vacations and hangs out, or a lazy person into someone ambitious or a self-centered individual into someone less selfish. When that doesn't happen, you keep right on trying—with the same frustrating result.

You underestimate your options and choices. You believe that you are helpless in a situation where you actually do have power. You think that you have no control at all, whether in attracting members of the opposite sex, finding the right job, or dealing with your boss. Feeling overwhelmed by circumstances, you tell yourself, "I don't have the education to get the job, so why bother to go to the interview" or "With my fat legs, I'll never meet anyone at this party."

The reality is, there are many events that you can try to take charge of, such as your intimate relationships, investments, and business dealings. Then there are times when you have virtually no control. Obviously, you have no control over a car jumping the curb and crashing into you, but fortunately, such random events are rare. Most of the time you have at least some power to protect yourself—and to advance your own interests. The task is to clarify which situations you can realistically influence and which ones you cannot. Only then can you begin to problem solve.

The Dangers of This BlindSpot

Thinking you have too little or too much control puts you at risk financially, personally, and professionally. The *Not Knowing When You're In or Out of Control* BlindSpot often works in tandem with *Wishful Thinking*, which intensifies its power.

When you exaggerate the extent of your power, you refuse to accept real limitations. This kind of thinking can ruin you. Imagine you're a retailer who keeps expanding into neighboring states. Dreaming of going national and overly impressed with your business savvy, you continue to open new stores, ignoring hikes in rent and insurance premiums, problems with creditors, and brutal new competition. You feel invulnerable, and you can't understand how precarious your situation really is and how rapidly the whole enterprise is falling apart. Finally your business collapses. We read stories in the newspapers about overexpansion all the time.

The flip side of this BlindSpot is underestimating or abdicating power and control. This, too, can be devasting. Because you feel impotent, you cede key life decisions to others, allowing them to make choices for you, such as what career path to follow. You may stay stuck in situations that make you desperately unhappy. The result is an unfulfilled life and/or the potential for unconscious rebellion and self-destructive acting out.

What's Behind This BlindSpot

Control is a central issue for everyone. We are all vulnerable. Life is very uncertain. You can take a plane and get hijacked. You may be rejected or betrayed in relationships. The boss may not like you. What saves you from paralysis is the *illusion of control*—the ability to live your life despite the threats around you. The illusion of control allows you to function as a normal human being. Without it, you'd become hyperaware of your vulnerability. If you really thought about everything that might happen when you drive a car, you'd never get behind the wheel. Since driving is a necessity, you have to adjust your sense of reality about what you can and can't control in order to go on with your life. Trouble starts when your illusion of control is distorted.

Key Elements of This BlindSpot

The *Not Knowing When You're In or Out of Control* BlindSpot is fueled by:

Focus on shortcomings. You undermine your confidence by dwelling on your weaknesses and minimizing your assets. Each of us carries a bundle of awareness patterns about ourselves, the people we deal with, and the situations we must negotiate. These patterns affect our perception of reality and out ability to predict how people will behave and how events will unfold. When you regularly perceive yourself in a negative way, you blind yourself to your strengths and let helpless feelings immobilize you. This kind of thinking prevents you from seeing your possibilities.

If you're a smoker, for example, you may think cigarettes control you and convince yourself that you're unable to give them up. Common self-talk runs, "I can't do it. I'll go out of my mind." Although cigarette smoking *is* an addiction, it's one that many people kick. If you're highly motivated, you're often capable of accomplishing more than you realize.

Grandiosity. Your view of reality is distorted by grandiosity, an inflated estimation of your power, value, knowledge, or importance. Grandiosity assures you that you can achieve far more than you really can, and leads you to ignore real dangers. For example, you buy an electrical supply company thinking you can reduce the hours you're open and eliminate emergency service without losing business. You think you've got things under control and that the company's excellent reputation is enough to carry you, even though customers keep complaining. Eventually they go elsewhere. Grandiosity is also a way of denying your vulnerability. For example, you've always had trouble managing people, yet you apply for a job as a supervisor. You rationalize, "This time I can do it," although you've repeatedly failed in the past—and nothing else has changed. You haven't enrolled in a management course or taken other steps to improve your skills. Although extending your reach is a positive goal, there's a line between striving to advance and grandiosity. It's grandiosity when you haven't learned from experience.

Life is very uncertain, and there is nothing you can do about that. But you can exercise the power you do have and benefit from the full range of possibilities in life. You can also get in touch with your limitations to assure your well-being.

Overcoming *Not Knowing When You're In or Out of Control*

Most of us have multiple opportunities to direct our lives. The question is, will the *Not Knowing When You're In or Out of Control* BlindSpot get in the way? To deal with this BlindSpot, follow the five steps of the Foolproof Plan. This process will help you spot any misperceptions you have about control, explain how they are causing (or have caused) flawed decisions, and help you avoid heartache in the future.

Step 1. *Focus on your objective.*

Know your goal. Don't lose sight of it, whether it's to lighten your workload, get a girlfriend, or change careers. If you're not achieving your goal, you've lost focus or the situation has changed. In either case you need to reassess what you're doing.

If your goal is an engagement ring from the man you've been living with for four years, and there's no proposal in sight, your strategy of waiting hopefully isn't working. You need to shift gears. He isn't going to marry you, and you need to make a choice: either accept him as a lover—or leave, which frees you to look for someone else who can give you what you want. Whatever you decide, at least you won't be fooling yourself.

Maybe your goal is getting your mate to handle the checkbook (or help with the baby)—and that isn't happening. Is your behavior working against you? If you constantly stand over your spouse, criticizing the way he or she accomplishes the task, you aren't going to get cooperation. You have to trust that someone else will do the job well enough, even if it's not up to your standards. If your mate gives up and hands the task back to you, you've gained nothing except resentment.

Your goal may be unrealistic. Figure out how much control you actually have in achieving your objective. You can't turn your child into a ballet dancer or rocket scientist unless he or she has the talent and interest. You can't fulfill your dream of being a firefighter if you can't meet the minimum physical requirements. *Beware of short-changing yourself, however.* You can't make someone else love you, but you can control whether you remain in a relationship that isn't good for you. It's also common to have a realistic goal, yet think your dream isn't achievable because you haven't thought it through.

It's hard to stop and ask yourself whether over- or underestimating your capabilities is stopping you from looking at other choices and options. Do it nevertheless.

Step 2. *Separate fact from fantasy.*

Make reality-based decisions instead of choices based on distorted thinking. Misperceptions about control can make the facts seem bleaker or brighter than is justified. For example:

Your version is: I can make my workaholic mate change his schedule and spend more time with me and our family.
The fact is: Asking someone else to change is a very tall order, even when there is love in a relationship and the other person genuinely wants to behave differently. Our underlying personalities don't change very much. We all need to able to influence our partner, but pressuring him/her to change only triggers anger. In reaction, the other person grows more determined to remain the same. The best you can do is change yourself.

Your version is: I can't get a girl because I'm a short, average-looking guy.
The fact is: You're funny, clever, and a good listener who makes women feel good about themselves. They're attracted to these qualities in you. Recognize your assets and stop comparing yourself to other men who are taller, better looking, or more macho—only to find that you don't measure up in *those* areas.

Your version is: My goal is to become president of my professional organization. I'll win the election because I'm a nice guy and I've been around a long time.
The fact is: You overestimate your appeal. A candidate with a stronger vision and better diplomatic skills is running against you. Beef up your own program and lobby the membership for support, or you're going to lose.

Use the assessment tools in chaper 6 to help sort out the facts.

Step 3. Recognize and remove emotional roadblocks.

Be alert to grandiosity and other obstructions that block you from progressing toward your goal, such as:

Dwelling on vulnerabilities. Refocus and change your perceptions of your weaknesses. Fortunately, you can learn to change distorted perceptions and form a realistic picture of what is achievable in any situation.

If you dwell on the perception that you're undesirable because you're 5'3" tall, you may wrongly assume women won't go out with you and miss out on a rich social life with meaningful female companionship.

Reframe your shortcomings. To see what we mean by reframing, take a look at real estate ads. A wreck is described as a "handyman's special." "Charming" is a code word for "small." "Modern kitchen" means old and outdated; otherwise the description would read "just renovated" or "brand-new."

Now, to expand your view of yourself, write a personals ad. Articulate your best qualities and ask a friend to help you. When you describe yourself, think a little differently and recast negatives to become positives. For example, substitute the word "cute" for "short" in your ad. Say, "I'm cute and a good listener." Describe yourself as "fit" and "a wrestler," which telegraphs visions of solid strength, not height. Run your ad past others to see if the description captures the essence of who you are. You usually have many more strengths and much more control than you assume. Many women hear a man is shy and think, "He's sensitive."

The same approach works when your negatives are job related. "Fifty-five-year-old executive" can become "Experienced executive with strong track record."

In another exercise, try to imagine how you would act if you were a handsome six-footer. Would you walk into a room smiling and confidant? Then model your behavior on that scenario. It may seem artificial and forced at first, but it will soon become a natural part of you. We all know men and women who are not at all impressive looking at first, yet because they have self confidence, they become attractive.

Feeling overwhelmed. One aspect of the *Not Knowing When You're In or Out of Control* BlindSpot is feeling so anxious and hopeless that you can't function. The solution: compartmentalize. This allows you to cut off feelings of impotence in one area of your life—put them in a "box" and forget about them so to speak—so you can function more efficiently in another area. If a part of your life is painful (as in cases of illness or unhappy relationships)—and there isn't anything you can do about it—it's very positive to take control and compartmentalize. For example, imagine your thirty-one-year-old son is adrift. He works at temporary office jobs, has no serious relationships with women, and you worry about him constantly. You're so preoccupied with this "black cloud" that you can't enjoy activities with the rest of your family. Put your worry into a compartment, then close it, so you can achieve pleasure and satisfaction in other areas. You can still think of ways to support your child, but creative problem-solving is different from chronic obsessing. All the worry in the world can't help your son—and it disables you.

Mistrust. If you can't delegate, you probably don't really want to give up control. You believe you can do a better job. But so what? Do you want help or not? The fact is, you need to stop interfering and criticizing at home and at the office. If someone is really incompetent, you'll know it soon enough.

Step 4. *Ask for feedback to inspire positive change.*

Seek advice. If you don't know when you're in or out of control, you're a poor judge of whether your goals or actions are realistic. You need to turn to outside resources. Before applying for a supervisory position, the same kind of job you've repeatedly failed at, talk to friends, trusted coworkers, whoever knows you and the situation well enough to provide informed feedback. Ask not only, "What are the chances I can get this position?" but also "What can I do to boost the odds of success?" One suggestion might be taking management seminars to improve your skills.

Take a Past Performance Inventory. This assessment uses your own feedback to identify what has worked for you before and where you've failed. (See chapter 6.) Use the inventory to evaluate your capabilities and play to your strengths. That's where success lies.

Step 5. *Act in your best interests.*

Recognize your power. In most situations, you do have a degree of power. You have to play the hand you're dealt, but you have some choice in how you play the game. The conviction that you're not smart enough or popular enough or that you're too old to make new friends or be successful holds you back. When you insist, "It's too late to change or try something new," it's important to challenge that assumption. The reality is: it's rarely too late. People can launch careers, start businesses, and make new friends at any time in their lives.

Make well-reasoned choices. When you take a risk, always ask yourself, "If the worst happens, can I tolerate it?" It's a difficult process, but your well-being depends on feeling that you have choices. Then if your decision doesn't work out, you don't feel like a victim because you exercised control.

Maybe you don't trust your feelings enough to know what's right for you. You succumb to family pressure to become a pharmacist because that's what your father and grandfather did. Then you wind up miserable because you never considered whether that career suits your skills or personality. Such situations demand conscious, well-reasoned choices, rather than automatically going along with someone else's suggestion. Consider whether there are other career paths you want to explore. Weigh the consequences of standing up to pressure—your own unhappiness versus the possibility of your parents' anger and rejection. Then decide what is more important to you: exploring another vocation and finding your own fulfillment—or family approval.

Ask "What am I willing to give up?" Maybe you want to be a stand-up comic. Giving up a regular paycheck may be out of the question, but working at clubs on weekends may be doable. If you want to change careers but don't have the experience you need, giving up time to volunteer might help you get what you want. You can learn to write speeches, run fundraising events, or gain other skills doing unpaid work for a nonprofit.

Know when to surrender. Recognize that there are some areas that you will never be able to control and know when to back off. If you believe you can control how your kids think and what they become, you are setting yourself up for a letdown. The fact is, you have little influence on a youngster's athletic ability, interests, career choice, or sexual orientation. If you continue to push a child in a direction where there is no aptitude or interest, you risk damaging your relationship. There is a difference between exerting your influence and micromanaging. If you overcontrol, you may win—your spouse or kids may acquiesce. But then they rebel. They may sneak around to do or get what they want.

The belief that you will never meet anybody else often blocks surrender to the reality of a dead-end relationship. When friends suggest, "Look around some of the online dating sites," you answer: "No, whoever is there is going to be a loser." Passivity sets in and you don't take charge. Remember: You often have to push yourself in ways that make you uncomfortable in order to achieve your objective.

A Classic Case of *Not Knowing When You're In or Out of Control*

The *Not Knowing When You're In or Out of Control* BlindSpot arises in a wide variety of situations. The story of Leo, a fifty-nine-year-old city planner, is a classic illustration of how this BlindSpot plays out. Leo sat in his kitchen one Saturday afternoon, nursing a Budweiser and swapping jokes with two of his best friends who had stopped by. The next day, he was dead of a massive stroke—and a fatally misguided illusion of control. His death was a tragedy that should not have happened.

Leo had a frightening family history of hypertension (high blood pressure). His father had died of a stroke in his fifties. Several cousins and his sister and brother were being treated for high blood pressure. Again and again, Leo's siblings urged him, "You've got to get checked. You've probably got it, too, and you may need medication."

Leo was terrified of doctors and hadn't seen one in thirty-five years. He listened politely to his family's concerns, then ignored the advice. Instead, he took daily vitamins and natural preparations purported to help lower blood pressure. Leo thought he could control a life-threatening condition all by himself, without medical assistance. He told his frightened wife and family, "I don't need a doctor. I don't need medication. I can treat myself."

Leo's goal was like anyone else's—staying healthy and living a long life. However, he thought he was in control of his own body and ignored the following facts:

- His family history put him at especially high risk for hypertension.
- Just because he felt fine didn't mean his blood pressure was normal. High blood pressure deserves the name "the silent killer" because it often has no symptoms. Yet it increases risk of heart attack and stroke.
- Effective treatments are available, but professional medical attention is essential.

Leo convinced himself that because he felt all right, nothing bad would happen. Further, he refused to listen to the objective counsel of others. His control BlindSpot worked in tandem with wishful thinking to literally kill him. It blocked his ability to recognize his lack of medical expertise and reinforced his decision to be his own doctor.

Leo's gender and stage of life played a role in his senseless death. Men are far less likely than women to see a physician. And although doctor-phobia probably won't put you in very much danger in your thirties—most people don't die of strokes or heart attacks that young—refusal to see a physician in middle age courts disaster.

Power Up

Trying to control what you can't control wastes time and energy, causes deep disappointment, and may even kill you. Passivity limits your social and professional success and general happiness. The answer is finding a balance. When you maximize the power you do possess, life becomes much easier and a sense of well-being more attainable. People often think, "If I had more money or success or a better body, all my problems would be solved." But happiness does not depend on having any one thing. There are always others, who are poorer, less attractive, or less capable than you are, who feel quite content. Capitalize on what you *do* have, rather than make excuses and dwell on what's missing. How you feel depends to a large extent on how you view your situation. You can choose to be satisfied or not.

CHAPTER 9

BlindSpot #3: Believing in Myths

I could never die for my beliefs because I may be wrong.

—BERTRAND RUSSELL

TO FIND OUT IF YOU HAVE THE *Believing in Myths* BLINDSPOT, RATE each statement below as follows:

1 = disagree most of the time
2 = disagree some of the time
3 = agree and disagree about equally
4 = agree some of the time
5 = agree most of the time

__ I make assumptions without sufficiently questioning their basis.
__ I believe in social and cultural myths.
__ I have a hard time adjusting to change.
__ I am a traditional person.
__ I've never challenged or thought much about long-held beliefs in my family.
__ TOTAL

Your score and what it means:

20–25: *Believing in Myths* is a major problem.

15–19: You have some serious myth problems.

8–14: A few issues need attention.

7 or less: You have little or no problem with myths.

Any score above 7 means you accept myths without examining or questioning them.

Understanding this BlindSpot

The *Believing in Myths* BlindSpot is at work when you're living your life by myths you've never examined. This BlindSpot explains why you never get the credit you deserve or why coworkers sabotage you, why your sex life is disappointing, or even why your kids get the worst teachers. Myths are unquestioned beliefs such as these:

If you're honest and play by the rules, so will everybody else.

Happy couples never fight.

You can get anything you want if you're willing to work hard enough.

Such myths are passed on from one generation to another through sayings or bits of folklore. The problem is, when you've got the *Believing in Myths* BlindSpot, you think that myths offer irrefutable wisdom and guidance. The truth is, many of them have little basis in fact. If you blindly follow their advice, you're headed for disappointment.

Myths run rampant in personal, financial, and business dealings. They seem harmless enough, but they stop you from facing important concerns, and perpetuate destructive behavior patterns. Myths blind you to factors or changes in your environment that require you to protect yourself, be effective, or advance your own interest. When these so-called truths are accepted without challenge, they support *Wishful Thinking*.

Many myths are part of our society and culture, such as, "If at first you don't succeed, try, try again." Although persistence is certainly important to success, it is not, by itself, enough. If you keep repeating the same actions that haven't worked in the past, you're likely to fail again. You must be able to figure out how to work *more effectively* the next time, perhaps by switching to a different strategy.

The belief that "You can be anything you want" may also disappoint. The idea that anyone can be president seems to be a particularly American cultural myth. The truth is there are very real limitations in this society, and you can't be absolutely anything you want. To a certain extent, you are in charge of the skills you acquire. But you can't control whether you are scientifically gifted and possess the hand-eye coordination to become a surgeon. You can't control whether you are beautiful enough to be a model, or whether you have the personality to become a TV talk show host or the talent to be a baseball star. Despite the myth of a level playing field, most people have to compromise.

Belief in myths about relationships distracts you from your goals and undermines your accurate assessment of yourself and others. Myth-based BlindSpots operate in a variety of relationship contexts, such as marriage, friendship, courtship, sex, and family interactions. Myths of the heart can be particularly cruel. The myth that "There's only one man (or woman) for me," suggests that if you lose that one person, you're destined to remain single for the rest of your life. There isn't just one perfect person for any of us. And someone who seems right for you at a particular time may be all wrong earlier or later in life. People can grow—or not.

The Dangers of This BlindSpot

Believing in myths is dangerous because it can get you fired, stop you from being promoted, lead your marriage into trouble, or hurt your family. Times have changed, and we live in a world that demands quick shifts in direction to meet new challenges. *Believing in Myths* discourages flexibility to deal with the changes around you. For example, you may never get promoted if your boss doesn't like you. It's probably in your best interest to transfer to another division where another supervisor will appreciate you. Yet belief in what your mother told you—the myth that good things come to those who wait—may keep you stuck, hoping your boss will change his attitude.

A very different type of myth involves the labeling of family members. It can be especially destructive because it stops you from exploring your full potential. One discrete characteristic, such as shyness, is often unconsciously used to define a whole person. Harry is the smart one; Billy is good with his hands; Mary has a great personality; June has no personality, but is athletic. Family members do have these characteristics, but usually they are also competent in other areas that are not appreciated. The shy person may also be a talented designer or a computer whiz or attuned to children.

Labeling can be especially damaging when your family prizes a characteristic that is not one of your strengths. For example, you may possess superior mechanical ability, but only average academic skills, in a family that values higher education and academic achievement. Being "good with your hands" may be looked down on or even sneered at. That's a very potent blow to your self-esteem.

There's a certain element of truth in all myths and fables or they wouldn't endure. But they're not the whole truth. Myths are often based on old truths or half truths that are no longer valid. Corporate chiefs may tell employees, "I like to think of us as one big family," but most people in a family don't turn on you or expect you to turn on other employees who are not functioning at high enough levels. Today the bottom line reigns. Anyone can be downsized—or have his or her jobs exported overseas—even those earning large salaries. Believing otherwise is a BlindSpot.

What's Behind This BlindSpot

Myths offer a familiar path to follow and a sense of security and predictability because you know how events will turn out. (If you're nice to people, people will be nice to you.) It's common to resist challenging myths because it's too painful *not* to believe in them. We all need *some* myths because life can be harsh and we have to solve difficult problems. Myths provide a certain comfort and reassurance. When you believe them literally, however, you get into trouble.

Key Elements of This BlindSpot

These behaviors support the *Believing in Myths* BlindSpot:

Magical thinking. Magical thinking is a variation of *Wishful Thinking* that blocks problem-solving.

For example, the belief that "love conquers all" implies that you and your partner can overcome all difficulties as long as you love each other. Unfortunately, love is not enough to sustain you through many of the obstacles two people face. Love does not banish unemployment or medical problems or misunderstandings. You need patience, communication skills, and luck to deal with adversity. This myth denies that you have to struggle in life and that there are limitations to the power of love.

There's nothing wrong with fantasizing that in the end you will win the girl and be happy. We need a certain amount of escape to function. However, balance is necessary. It's when you lose perspective and think escape is reality that you cross the line into trouble.

Stubbornness, resistance to change, unrealistic expectations. These factors stop you from acting in your own behalf. Maybe you find your children are always assigned to the least desirable teachers in their grade. You attribute it to bad luck and keep following the rules. Then you finally realize the children who get the best teachers have parents who approached the administration and made specific requests. The myth that life is fair misled you. Unless you ask for Mrs. Smith or Mr. Jones, too, your children will probably continue to draw less desirable teachers. The task is to separate what is true and useful in myths from what is not and avoid taking the easy way out, instead of facing and dealing with important issues.

Overcoming *Believing in Myths*

Are you taken in (and harmed by) myths? Follow the Foolproof Plan to identify myths that guide you, examine them with a clear eye, and stop them from causing problems in your personal or professional life.

Step 1. *Focus on your objective.*

Know your goal. Imagine you're a public-relations executive who brings in large amounts of new business. Your goal is to earn the salary you deserve and have a prestigious title on your door. Yet that isn't happening because you believe the myth that innovative ideas and great work will always be rewarded. Your strategy of passively waiting for recognition results in others taking credit for your accomplishments. It's time to switch gears and blow your own horn.

Maybe your goal is to have a happy marriage. Because you believe the myth, "Happily married couples don't fight," your strategy is to avoid any conflict. Your mate has walked out on you anyway. "We had such a wonderful relationship. I don't remember having a single argument," you boast. But your belief has misled you. There is no rule about how often spouses are supposed to fight. Yet when a couple *never* argues, that's a sure sign of trouble. Marriage is messy. No matter how much you love each other, if you're human you're going to disagree at times, whether it's about finances or the children or in-laws. It's impossible for two people to always see things the same way. You need to think realistically about what constitutes a happy marriage for you and work with your partner toward that goal, understanding that there will inevitably be conflicts that will need to be worked through.

Or perhaps your goal is to be happy on the holidays, just like everyone else you see in magazine and TV ads at Christmas or Thanksgiving. Instead you feel depressed and as if you're the only one in the world with a dysfunctional family. In this case, you need a more realistic goal: finding a meaningful way to celebrate the holidays. To achieve it, ask, "What can I do differently to make this a more pleasant occasion for me?

Step 2. *Separate fact from fantasy.*

Replace blind belief in myths with realistic evaluation.

> *Your version:* People will do the right thing. It's unseemly to crow about your own achievements.
> *The fact is:* People often do the *wrong* thing because it's easier. Again and again, you do the legwork to win business. Then a colleague marches up to you, gives you a hug—and takes the credit. The partners in your firm don't know how effective you are. When they ask, "Who worked on the project?" your name is never mentioned. Modesty may have worked in your family, but it takes assertiveness and the ability to promote yourself to get ahead in a competitive environment.

> *Your version:* If my husband loved me, he'd know what I want.
> *The fact is:* This myth leads you to expect others to read your mind. Women frequently contend, "If I have to tell him what turns me on or what would be a special Valentine's Day gift, it spoils the romance. He should know enough to buy me a bottle of perfume or send flowers." But you often don't know what someone else wants even if you love the person. The individual may have to tell you over and over again. What's your goal? To have a lovely day or to cling to a myth?

> *Your version:* I hate the holidays. There's always family tension. Why can't my Christmas and Thanksgiving be as joyful as they are for everyone else?
> *The fact is:* Hospital emergency rooms are filled with depressed people at Christmas. "Why am I feeling so lousy?" the patients ask. "Everyone is supposed to feel good during the holidays." There's actually a lot you can do to create a more meaningful holiday experience. If Christmas dinner is always tense, change the venue. Host it at your house where *you're* in control, instead of at your mother's.

Or change the mix of people; invite friends along with your grating father-in-law. Or change dinner to a brunch, which makes it more casual. Holidays are happy for some people. If that's not true for you, stop bemoaning that you don't have the best family relationships. Think of ways to have a better time and get more out of the holidays.

Step 3. Recognize and remove emotional roadblocks.

These factors stand in the way of happiness and fulfillment:

Unreasonable expectations. There's the myth that it's important for you and your partner to have orgasms at the same time. If that doesn't happen, you may feel that something is wrong with your sex life. But making love is not a task to be accomplished; it's a process of relating to another person. What's relevant is that both of you experience pleasure, not whether you climax simultaneously.

Fear. Fear of exposing cracks in a marriage that can't be repaired often causes couples to paper over disagreements and make believe they don't exist. If that's your strategy, you can't discuss issues and problem solve. You may feel frustrated by an unimaginative sex life and your mate's inattentativeness. Your spouse may feel taken for granted and unappreciated for the long hours he or she works. Discussion of these resentments generates tension and disequilibrium in the short term, but it's a starting point for improved communication and a revitalized marriage.

Brainwashing. Family labeling myths can cause great damage. People get pigeonholed by these myths until they grow to believe the labels themselves. If you're told that you don't have an ear for music, you probably won't try to play an instrument. When you repeatedly hear "You're no good in English," you're probably not going to try to write well. If your brother is the smart one and you're the handsome one, you're not going to get a Ph.D. He is.

Ask yourself, "Are my choices and my view of myself based on my own experiences or what other people have told me?" Recognize how being told that you aren't good at arithmetic or at sports limits you in your present life. Playing the piano can bring a lot of pleasure, whether or not you're talented.

Step 4. Ask for feedback to inspire positive change.

If you're not being recognized in your career, talk to trusted coworkers for their view of what's going on. Be prepared to hear that you need to speak up for yourself, even though that is not good news. Take a look, too, at how others handle situations similar to yours successfully and learn from them. Do colleagues ask for promotions—and get them? What do they do that you don't? Do other couples fight, make up, and enjoy a good relationship? Observe their techniques.

To realistically assess your abilities and whether family labeling has shortchanged you, ask friends and others you trust for their opinion. They can be more objective than you are about your multiple competencies. Learn from role models and reality checks.

Step 5. Act in your best interests.

Identify the myths that tend to guide you. Do any of the myths mentioned in this chapter have a negative impact on your personal or professional life? Can you think of other strongly held beliefs that cause difficulties for you? There's no way to ignore all the myths that you grew up with, but you can examine them with a clear eye when facing new situations and ask, "Is this really true?"

Beware of labeling others. Are you unwittingly limiting the potential of your own children or other family members? You may want to highlight certain of your child's talents, but beware of labeling him or her in a way that discourages exploration of other interests and talents, too. Yes, Johnny may draw wonderful cartoons, but he may also ice skate like a pro or excel at debating or chess. Be just as careful about labeling friends or relatives in any way that obscures or minimizes the other aspects of who they are.

Be honest with yourself. Have you been misled by myths—or have you really taken the easy way out to avoid facing important issues? If you insist that your boss should offer a raise for your hard work (and you shouldn't have to ask for it), you may *really* mask a fear of being turned down. Or maybe your dream is to be a playwright. You automatically accept the belief that "You can't earn a living in the arts"—and use it as an excuse to avoid risking failure. In fact, if you really want to write, you can get up an hour earlier every day and write before you go to work. Even if you can't earn a living from writing, you can enjoy it.

Stop doing more of the same. Think and act differently. Instead of working the same old way in your job and not getting what you want, pay attention to the nature of relationships in your organization. Learn who are the bosses and what are their goals? Who can help you in the company? Ask yourself, "Where will I be in a year if I continue to do what I'm doing."

A Classic Case of *Believing in Myths*

Many people are taken in and harmed by work- or career-related myths. These myths play out in a variety of ways. A classic case is fifty-one-year-old David. David had been chair of the history department in a large Southern university for over ten years when a new president was appointed. The president promised to look into how efficiently the various departments were run and make whatever cuts and other changes he deemed necessary. Although everyone thought of David as an extremely nice person and a diligent worker, it was well known that he was one of the department chairs in danger of losing his position.

David had been raised in a strict, religious family, where his parents emphasized the importance of trust and taught their children that if you work hard you will succeed. David took this piece of folk wisdom quite literally.

After David became a department head, he thought he had reached the pinnacle of his career, and he started working harder than ever. No detail was too small for him. As a consequence, instead of dealing with important problems, he bombarded his colleagues with paperwork that wasted everyone's time and made people angry.

Professors who were jealous of David's power sought out the new president as soon as he arrived. They presented an unflattering picture of him. Aware of the behind-the-scenes maneuvering, David's closest friend and colleague warned him, "Your approach isn't working. Rumors are flying that you're going to be asked to leave. You need to make radical changes in your management style." David scoffed at the advice, responding, "I haven't heard any of those rumors."

By the time David realized his position was precarious, it was already too late. But that didn't stop him from trying to save his job by working even more diligently. It never occurred to David that all his hard work was irrelevant to the situation. Instead of impressing the president, it only served to strengthen the president's feeling that David couldn't improve his management or communication skills, or become an effective problem solver.

Brought down by new leadership and old resentments, David lost his chair. Sadly, he never understood the reasons for his demotion. Even after months of reflection, he didn't realize that there were more effective ways he might have protected himself. For example, he could have presented his case to the president and emphasized his accomplishments before others had a chance to spotlight his failures. He could have stopped trusting people who were undermining him.

David continues to blame his demotion on an unjust action by uncaring administrators, considering it one of those arbitrary occasions when evil conquers good. To this day, he remains blinded by belief in the ultimate value (and triumph) of hard work and good intentions. *Believing in Myths* stopped him from focusing on his goal—keeping his job—and changing his strategy.

Many myths lead us to act self-destructively. Some myths stem from ideas or behavior models that may have worked for a time, but have now grown unproductive. Hard work alone may have counted more when most people farmed or earned their living through other kinds of manual labor. Today the world values those who work smart, not hard. It isn't only the amount of work you do, it's the nature of the work that pays dividends.

Turn on the Light

Hidden cultural and family beliefs all have a strong influence on your actions. They may sabotage your happiness, undermine your goals, and allow others to take advantage of you. Use your new awareness to halt myth mischief starting now.

CHAPTER 10

BlindSpot #4: Not Knowing How You Come Across

If there's a Mercedes in the driveway,
the price of painting the house doubles.

—ANONYMOUS PAINTING CONTRACTOR

TO FIND OUT IF YOU HAVE THE *Not Knowing How You Come Across* BlindSpot, rate each statement below as follows:

1 = disagree most of the time
2 = disagree some of the time
3 = agree and disagree about equally
4 = agree some of the time
5 = agree most of the time

__ I have trouble making and keeping friends in my private life and at work.

__ I am not aware of the impression I make socially and professionally.

__ I find it hard to read other people.

__ I often don't know what behavior is expected of me.

__ It is difficult to keep my eye on my goal and I get sidetracked easily.

__ TOTAL

Your score and what it means:

20–25: *Not Knowing How You Come Across* is a major problem.

15–19: You have some serious coming-across issues.

8–14: A few issues need attention.

7 or less: You have little or no problem with knowing how you come across.

Any score above 7 means that, even though you're not aware of it, you misjudge the image you project.

Understanding This BlindSpot

The *Not Knowing How You Come Across* BlindSpot—misperceiving how you appear to others—makes it difficult to navigate the relationships in your life and get what you want. It explains why you don't get promoted (or hired in the first place), why people don't send you new business, why you can't meet a girl or a guy, and why coworkers are cool or stir up trouble. This BlindSpot distorts your view of the image you project with the opposite sex, your boss, prospective clients, your family, and anyone else who is important to you. It has three components:

Blindness to yourself. You're unaware of your own behavior and the negative response it provokes in others. For example, you perceive yourself as sensitive and easygoing, when your wife finds your yelling scary and intimidating. Men who erupt in anger out of feelings of helplessness or frustration are often stunned to learn their families see them very differently. People in general tend to minimize the effect of uncontrolled anger on others, but it is usually more hurtful than the angry person realizes. Or you think you're dedicated and friendly, when other members of your book group see you as shallow and snobbish because you're always name-dropping. Or maybe you think no one notices that you constantly make personal phone calls at work. Because you don't realize the effect you have and how people perceive you, you don't get ahead or get along—at work and when trying to build a meaningful social or home life.

Blindness to other people's agendas. You miss other people's signals, their motives, and their BlindSpots. For all the talk about team effort, there is always a great deal of internal competition on the job. Just because your mother is proud of you doesn't mean others are thrilled at your latest success. It's not unusual for certain people to look for opportunities to trip you up—or prejudge you on superficial evidence—but you're oblivious to the need for self-protection. Although envy may not be an admirable emotion, it is human nature to feel disgruntled when seeing someone else win a big title or get accepted at Harvard Business School. Other people's envy is particularly strong when they perceive you as already having more than your share of good fortune—or if you flaunt your success.

And of course, envy arises insidiously in social situations, as well. If you live in the biggest house in town, you're probably going to be a target for envy.

Blindness to the role of "context." There are times when you *want* to look successful and intimidate people—and times when that approach undermines you. If you're a lawyer who wishes to impress important clients, your interests are advanced by a fancy office and expensive suits. When your clients are working-class people, a luxurious office might scare them away.

Knowledge of context is especially critical when you're looking for a job. What constitutes an appropriate and positive appearance at interviews depends in part on the position and the field involved. Nose rings, visible body piercings, or purple hair may not put you at a disadvantage if you're auditioning for a rock group or applying for a job in a music store—but they are likely to turn off interviewers in most other businesses. If you want to manage a bank, sell stocks in suburbia, or enter a profession, you're more likely to get called back if you play it safe and make a conservative appearance.

The Danger of This BlindSpot

This BlindSpot is dangerous because it ruins careers and relationships with people you care about. In extreme cases, it can get you fired and lead to actionable charges against you. For example, most sexual harassment cases have nothing to do with actual sex. Rather, they are caused by supervisors (usually male) whose conscious or unwitting behavior creates an oppressive workplace for their female employees. The employees complain they can't work because they are continually harassed.

Maybe you're a supervisor who struts around the office saying, "Hey babe, you look really good today," or making off-color remarks. You think you're "just having fun," being cute or clever, and giving compliments. But if you're blind to the many hints from your employees that you are acting inappropriately, you could wind up charged with sexual harassment. This kind of behavior leads women to quit and file lawsuits. Even if you save your job, your reputation will probably dash any hopes of career advancement. Management does become aware of people who aren't promotion material.

Seeing yourself as others see you is important in all situations, but obviously it's more critical in some than others. The BlindSpot may not only destroy relationships with people you love, but also cause unintended consequences. One man almost died because his booming voice when he was angry cowed his wife into obedience. Although he had signs of internal bleeding for days, he angrily forbade her to call the doctor. He was afraid he'd have to go to the hospital. Fortunately, she finally found the courage to trust her own judgment. She notified their physician, who immediately sent the man to the emergency room. By this time, he had lost so much blood he required a transfusion. While lying in his hospital bed, he thanked his wife for saving his life. As they talked, he was stunned to realize how close he had come to dying and how intimidated she felt by his bluster.

What's Behind This BlindSpot

If you're like most of us, you tend to be blind to your own shortcomings. You're probably taken aback when you see or hear yourself on tape for the first time, and respond, "I had no idea that I looked/sounded like that." It's common to feel shocked when a similar technique is used in therapy and self-awareness groups—and other participants tell you how you come across. There is often little correlation between how you see yourself and how you appear to others.

It's easy to succumb to this BlindSpot because it soothes your anxiety. When you don't know how you come across, you don't have to worry about how you look or what you say or do. In truth, ignorance *can* be bliss—and to a certain extent it's helpful. There are some things you can't do anything about. If you've got a limp that can't be corrected, you're stuck with it. It's positive not to dwell on it. But it's easy to cross the line into self-defeating behavior and fool yourself. There's usually a great deal you can do about making a good impression.

Wearing a rumpled suit and shoes that need a shine can hurt you at a job interview. "When you aren't concerned enough about appearance, it conveys the impression that you are not a professional. This conclusion extends to, 'He's unlikely to do a good job for us because he doesn't care about details,'" says Kathy Sanborn, a life and career coach in Sacramento, California.

Key Elements of This BlindSpot

These destructive dynamics are at work when you misperceive how you come across:

Self-Centered Thinking

Before you can cope with other people's reactions to you, you need to see things from their perspective, however limited or inaccurate that perspective might be. Self-centered thinking works against that, as does *denial* that your behavior puts people off—or that others are competitive with you and you need to watch your back. It's a mistake to underestimate the power of envy in any situation in which you are successful.

Self-Serving Perceptions

You're certain the problem is theirs, not yours. In your own mind, you didn't get the promotion because the boss showed favoritism toward another employee. As a result, you never examine your contribution to failing to get what you want—your reputation as someone who can't keep a confidence and spreads gossip at the water cooler.

Confirmation Bias

This is the tendency to look for, and cling to, evidence that confirms your beliefs. You ignore or undervalue the relevance of contradictory information. For example, you may believe that all your employees admire and respect you, based on a single piece of information that tends to confirm your hypothesis—and discard other clear evidence of the animosity many workers actually harbor toward you. If your spouse points out that you put down your receptionist and yelled at the mail clerk, you counter defensively with "Pete and June think I'm a great boss."

This type of self-deception resembles one of the techniques psychics use to deceive their customers. The charlatan rattles off twenty observations or predictions about your life. If one or two of those are what you want to believe, you tend to ignore the other statements you would otherwise consider inaccurate. In confirmation bias, however, you're your own charlatan."

Overcoming *Not Knowing How You Come Across*

In general, it's a good idea to know the impression you make on other people—and to understand the motivations and reactions of other people—in order to succeed in the world. These skills become crucial when you're having difficulty on the job, at home, or elsewhere in your life and need to take action to help yourself. Follow the five-step

Foolproof Plan below to analyze what's holding you back and "read" yourself and others more accurately. This process also helps you modify behavior that limits you and expand your possibilities.

Step 1. *Focus on your objective.*

Know your goal. Whether it's to meet someone new or succeed at your job, keep your objective in clear view. If you're not achieving your goal, you may have lost focus or your situation may have changed. You need to reassess what you're doing. Yes, it's hard to reevaluate, but it's necessary to get where you want to go.

If the goal is to become a top executive at your company—and you're not moving ahead—your strategy may be wrong, and you may have to change direction. Maybe you've been worried about stirring competition or looking too aggressive and have therefore become overly accommodating. You come across as passive rather than as an achiever who gets things done. Try another approach. If you want to move on the fast track, you have to look and act the part—and project a stronger, more aggressive image.

If your goal is to build an effective workforce, and valued people are leaving instead, your habit of yelling at and humiliating people is backfiring. You have to change your approach. Or perhaps you're a successful career woman who is divorced and wants to meet someone. Every time you introduce yourself to eligible men as a partner in your consulting firm, you find they immediately disappear. Your strategy of mentioning your credentials upfront obviously isn't working. Change your tactics.

Step 2. *Separate fact from fantasy.*

You can't deal with your BlindSpot unless you have an unobstructed view of reality. Separate concrete information from fiction.

> *Your version:* My competence as a teacher and my good intentions are all that matter in working harmoniously with colleagues at my

high school. My designer wardrobe and my BMW in the parking lot are irrelevant.
The fact is: That's not how the world works. The way you dress and the car you drive are statements that can have as much impact on the way you're perceived as the way you behave. If you think otherwise, you're fooling yourself.

Your version: If people don't perform effectively, they have to be told in no uncertain terms. So what if I yell?
The fact is: There are consequences for treating people badly, such as employee turnover and a sullen workforce.

Your version: I'll impress men by telling them I'm a partner in my company. They'll be attracted to a very successful woman.
The fact is: Many men feel threatened by powerful women. That's the reality, unpleasant as it may be. Accept it if your number-one goal is to get married. Instead of broadcasting your credentials, you might talk about other areas of your life until the "prospect" gets to know you. A deception? More of an omission, but one that probably won't do any harm.

Step 3. *Recognize and remove emotional roadblocks.*

These roadblocks take your eye off your goal or cloud your view of how you come across:

Stubbornly dwelling on what's fair or right. Your clothes and your car are very superficial things, but they can have a profound effect on what you want to accomplish. People often prejudge based on stereotypes about looks, financial status, and other factors. It isn't right, but it's reality. If you want a smooth relationship with your coworkers, especially when you're new on the scene, look at the situation from their perspective. That doesn't mean you agree with their point of view, but you do have to recognize it to protect yourself.

Anger. We tend to minimize the effect of uncontrolled anger on others, but it is usually hurtful. In the workplace, word travels fast about an angry management style. This kind of reputation can hurt you even if you're in a powerful position.

Insensitivity. You need empathic skills—the ability to understand someone else's feelings, circumstances, and motives—to make friends and keep them. It's also essential to read nonverbal cues, such as irritation in another person's voice or fatigue in body movement or facial expressions, so that you can respond appropriately.

Good manners, kindness, and recognition of the other person's needs are crucial to meaningful relationships. If you're a fitness trainer, realize that the hour is about the client and the workout, not about reporting on your social life.

Fear of looking too powerful. If you're afraid of igniting the envy of others, you'll hold back. Recognize that if you want to be successful and a leader, you're bound to be a target for some people. What if your success does upset someone? Is being liked worth being less effective than you can be? You may find that you can live with the envy of others and it won't destroy you.

Step 4. *Ask for feedback to inspire positive change.*

Sometimes you have a sense of what's getting in the way of reaching your goals. At other times, it's important to consult others to find out why you're not achieving your objective and whether you're sabotaging yourself.

Raise your awareness. You may not realize how arrogant, caustic, or sour you appear, and how that stops people from sharing important information with you or asking you to join important committees or projects. You may be unaware that you complain too much or are viewed as cheap because you don't pay your share of restaurant checks. Your life partner, who knows and loves you, or trusted friends, are good sources of information. Listen to their unsolicited input, instead of brushing it off.

Check your self-view. Do you think you're in line for a promotion when management is actually dissatisfied with you? Do you think you're doing a good sales job when you aren't even making quotas?

Do you have an overly optimistic view of your skills? To figure out how you're really doing, consult people who don't have an emotional investment in the situation. One way to find out if your self-view is accurate is to check in with your boss. Performance reviews and annual employee evaluation meetings are good forums for asking questions about areas in which you might improve. You may be surprised to learn that you don't do well as part of a team.

In creative fields like acting or modeling it's less clear how you're doing because there are no definite measurements like sales volume or the number of new clients you brought in. You may get rejected for roles or jobs and never know why. In such cases, try to ask a friend in the field for feedback.

Beware of confirmation bias. When you receive feedback, remember that the more threatened or insecure you feel, the more you ignore information that contradicts your beliefs.

Step 5. *Act in your best interests.*

Realize there's more than one way to express yourself. Be aware of the many facets of your personality and of the wide spectrum of effective ways you can behave. For example, if you want a promotion that requires leadership qualities, you can prepare yourself to appear stronger, more authoritative and decisive. It's important to increase the flexibility in your repertoire to take advantage of opportunities and respond to challenges.

Often this requires nothing more than acting the part—and a lot of rehearsal—certainly not a deep personality change. For example, you might need to practice "acting confident" in front of a mirror, then in front of an audience of your trusted friends. As one therapist colleague of ours put it, "Fake it till you make it."

Have a multidimensional view of yourself. You can be authoritarian and compassionate, confident, and empathetic. Knowing the variety of ways you can behave expands your options and effectiveness in any situation in which you interact with others, but especially in social situations.

Speak up. Tell others about the full range of your talents and abilities. If you want to be considered for a collaborative project, mention how well you work with others. They may not know about that asset. If you keep silent, you hold back important information that can change attitudes about you. There are times when you're called upon to act in a way that is different from the way you normally act.

Figure out what to change and do it. Do you get along with others in the workplace and build alliances with colleagues to get support? Or do you focus on rivalries and intense competition with peers, so that you're surrounded by people who want you to fail? Do you see success as dangerous and keep a low profile, undermining your own power?

Are you sometimes too blunt? Always consider the context and the strength of the relationship. Don't tell your boss he's doing a terrible job unless you're prepared to risk his wrath and possibly get fired. To build up your empathic skills, ask yourself, "If I were Tom, what would I want someone to say to me in this situation?"

Repair the damage. Apologies express regret for a fault or offense and often ask for pardon. They soothe ruffled feelings, heal relationships, and frequently change the way you come across. If you're worried that your remarks might have offended a friend or client, try, "I was wondering if you were upset by what I said." This statement gives you a reality check. Maybe your concern is unwarranted. But if you have caused pain, the statement gives the other person a chance to say, "Yes, I felt hurt." Then the two of you can talk about it. There is an opportunity to make amends and perhaps even strengthen the relationship. We all do and say things at times that we wish we hadn't. But damage control is often possible.

It can be embarrassing and awkward to apologize, which is why we may not do it as often as we should. Some of us find that email acts as a buffer that makes it easier to apologize. You can say exactly what you want without having to parry the other person's response. Once you've done the hard part—getting the "I'm sorry" out of the way—it's much easier to discuss things further.

A Classic Case of *Not Knowing How You Come Across*

The *Not Knowing How You Come Across* BlindSpot almost ruined the academic career of Pamela, a well-known biology professor we treated. Pamela won accolades and awards, was appointed to national panels, and traveled to conferences all over the world, regularly bringing in multimillion-dollar grants to her university. She considered herself a friendly person who maintained good relationships with colleagues and students—and thought she was well liked. But one day, without warning, Pamela was accused of falsifying time sheets for three work-study students. Although only a small amount of money was involved, she was accused of fraud. If found guilty, she not only would have lost her reputation, but also would have been banned from receiving government money. This would have destroyed her research career, which depended on grants. At least some of her colleagues took pleasure in her misfortune.

In all university cultures, there are certain spoken and unspoken requirements for the faculty. At Pamela's school, professors were expected to be seen around the campus. However, Pamela was often away on trips, which brought money and prestige to the university. Pamela underestimated how much her colleagues envied her work style or how far they would go to undermine her. She was unaware of frequent whispered comments, such as, "She's the phantom professor. She's so busy globe-trotting, she's never here."

Pamela's goal was a successful career. Yet due to her *Not Knowing How You Come Across* BlindSpot, she failed to recognize that competition, envy, and prejudice are facts of life in the workplace—and that you have to watch out for other people's emotional roadblocks, as well as your own. Her fantasy that she was popular and that her fund-raising efforts were universally appreciated was disastrously naïve in our status-conscious culture. She failed to anticipate and deflect resentment and prepare for possible political maneuvering against her. If she had, she might have helped herself by becoming more available and visible on campus. Even if she decided not to reduce her travel schedule, she would have been more prepared for the hostility toward her and the attempt to discredit her. She also might have made more of an effort to socialize with colleagues, since prejudices often dissipate when people get to know you better.

After an investigation that cost the university tens of thousands of dollars, Pamela was asked to pay back a total of $43 because of a mistake in addition. There wasn't even a hint of fraud. By this time, however, the episode had so embittered the atmosphere and soured Pamela's relationship with her supervisors that she felt squeezed out. She decided to seek a position elsewhere and is now at a university in another state.

Put Your Best Self Forward

The way you come across can get you where you want to go in life—or serve as a handicap. Do you have an image of yourself that is very different from what everyone else sees? Deal with your *Not Knowing How You Come Across* BlindSpot, and you gain much more control over your impact on others—and your life.

CHAPTER 11

BlindSpot #5: Looking for a Hero

Show me a hero and I will write you a tragedy.

—F. SCOTT FITZGERALD

TO FIND OUT IF YOU HAVE THE *Looking for a Hero* BLINDSPOT RATE each statement below as follows:

1 = disagree most of the time
2 = disagree some of the time
3 = agree and disagree about equally
4 = agree some of the time
5 = if you agree most of the time

__ I have a history of being attracted to charismatic people.
__ I frequently idealize someone, only to become disillusioned about him or her later on.
__ I look for situations where I can get something for nothing.
__ I trust my first impressions of people.
__ I tend to dismiss quiet people.
__ TOTAL

Your score and what it means:

20-25: The *Looking for a Hero* BlindSpot is a major problem.

14-19: You have serious issues in some areas.

8-13: Some issues need attention.

7 or less: You have little or no problem with *Looking for a Hero.*

Any score above 7 means you may be looking for a hero.

Understanding This BlindSpot

The *Looking For a Hero* BlindSpot—idealizing (and ascribing magical powers to) someone else—leads you to blindly entrust your fate to another individual in your personal, financial, or work life. You believe that the person has unique knowledge or expertise, and attach yourself to him or her, thinking you will become the beneficiary of that special power. In your mind, the hero will make your romantic dreams come true, protect you from harm, or make you rich. Inevitably you're disappointed when the hero turns out to be less than superhuman—or worse, a charlatan. You discover that your fiancé is already married or your new bathrooms cost triple the amount the contractor led you to believe or your fantastic new boss has manipulated you.

It's very tempting to "fall in love" with someone you perceive as a hero, which is why this BlindSpot is particularly pervasive in two hot-button areas: romance and money. In the romance department, many individuals have a deep-seated need to be taken care of by someone else—the more powerful the other person, the better. If you're a student, you fall for the professor; if you're an administrative assistant, you fall for the boss. Although a certain amount of idealization of the other person is part of any romance—he or she is "perfect," at least in the beginning—in this case the myopia goes too far.

In the financial sphere, the *Looking For a Hero* BlindSpot typically appears when you want to make lots of money and think you will become successful or raise your status by associating with the hero. We all need role models. But when you succumb to this BlindSpot, you choose the wrong people to admire, or you expect them to perform in areas beyond their expertise. Just because someone is a brilliant scientist doesn't mean this person will make a faithful husband or a fine wife.

The Dangers of This BlindSpot

This BlindSpot is dangerous because it makes you a willing dupe for financial or emotional con artists—or because you invest your idol with far more clout or ability than the individual actually possesses. In either case, you fail to reason properly and get hurt. Your devotion or adoration is often informed by very little evidence. You're blind to any flaws in the hero or what he is selling you because you're dazzled by his charisma. The trouble is, this person or project can draw you into legal, economic, or personal disasters.

Imagine you need an accountant, and you decide to go to a "CPA to the stars." His client list includes singers and actors who are household names. He maintains an impressive suite of offices and dresses like a rock star. New clients flock to him, despite his astronomical fees. The very idea of entering this glamorous world and having this kind of a heavyweight handle your taxes is too good an opportunity to pass up.

But your tax returns don't get the attention they require. In time you're audited by the IRS. Then you continue to get audited every three years. You were "small potatoes" to the accountant and not exactly at the top of his list of priorities. If you're a writer or actor, you may receive the same lack of attention from a big-name agent for the same reasons.

Not all heroes are glamorous, however. This BlindSpot is also costly when the hero is someone performing an important service for you, and you blindly follow the person's advice without examination.

What's Behind This BlindSpot

Behind this BlindSpot is the desire for a "superman" or "superwoman" who relieves you of the necessity to think for yourself. In romantic relationships, a hero may even assure "I know what's best for you." If you lack confidence or struggle with low self-esteem, you may find that comforting to hear. It's also very appealing to put yourself in someone else's hands in other situations, which is why your hero may be a financial advisor, lawyer, even a plumber or a computer consultant—anyone who has specialized skill in a subject or an area that is mysterious to you.

Hero worship surfaces when you lack the knowledge or expertise to cope with a problem or situation. You feel vulnerable and let the expert handle your problems. It's common to look for heroes when building or renovating a house. You feel overwhelmed because there are so many decisions to make in areas you know nothing about. So you jump at the offer when the architect you hire proposes, "Don't worry about a thing. I'll bring in and supervise the plumbers, electricians, and rest of the crew."

Similar scenarios arise when you have medical problems. It's understandable to want to be taken care of when you're sick. You may not bother to get a second or third opinion because you've already got an expert recommending a course of treatment. The self-talk runs, "He's the doctor. I didn't go to medical school." The same logic applies when you've got car trouble and think, "I'm not a mechanic."

There's nothing wrong with seeking out and relying on an expert—in fact that's the smart thing to do when you lack knowledge in a particular area. What causes problems is abdicating your own responsibility once you hire the person. If you forget that the expert works for you, and don't ask questions and monitor the situation, you're asking for trouble.

Key Elements of This BlindSpot

Intensely Positive Feelings

This is an immediate danger signal that might mean you're making judgments too quickly in your financial dealings, love life, and even in your friendships. Anytime you're overly impressed by someone the very first time you meet, be careful. Trust doesn't develop that way. Instant camaraderie with a new coworker or fellow PTA member is great, but remember that deeper relationships develop over time as they build a track record.

Illusion of Perfection

Because you want the hero to be authentic, you resist seeing fault lines. You blind yourself to knowledge that would diminish the hero's power over you. If the person has flaws, it rocks your plans and your security. The *Wishful Thinking* BlindSpot (see chapter 7) works right along with the *Looking for a Hero* BlindSpot to protect your illusion of perfection and your comfort level.

Vulnerability and Need for Reassurance

Women may be more vulnerable than men to the *Looking for a Hero* BlindSpot, after a painful divorce or the end of a love affair. Regardless of gender, this BlindSpot is activated when your self-esteem is at a low point and you want reassurance that you are still desirable. In this climate, you are more likely to ignore negative characteristics in another person that at another time might make you stop and think.

This BlindSpot is tough to overcome because you need to challenge what feels like natural, honest feelings about having a future with someone and your unwillingness to jeopardize what you perceive as your chance for happiness. The BlindSpot results when you block out information that points to breaking off a relationship. If you become blind, you don't see the signs that you're being deceived.

Overcoming *Looking for a Hero*

Someone else's personal magnetism or glamorous reputation can be hard to resist. Occasionally, the hero never even asked for or wanted the special status you've conferred. It's all *your* idea. But whether someone deliberately fools you or you deceive yourself, you need to learn to protect yourself. Follow the five-step Foolproof Plan below to recognize the *Looking For a Hero* BlindSpot and stop it in its tracks.

Step 1. Focus on your objective.

Know your goal. Keep your eye on it. Is your goal to get your tax returns handled competently and avoid IRS audits? Will using a celebrity accountant accomplish that any better than using a competent local CPA? It may impress your friends to be the celebrity accountant's client, but that isn't relevant to your goal. The question is, will he or she give you attention and excellent accounting services?

Maybe your goal is to attach yourself to a leader. Your new CEO promises to streamline the company and position it for growth. You agree to become his lieutenant and help reduce staff. But the situation changes. He uses an ax instead of a scalpel to cut personnel. Do you still want to be part of his team? You've bought into the CEO's goal without thinking through your own objective, a common occurrence when you have the *Looking For a Hero* BlindSpot. You lose the ability to separate what you want from what the hero wants.

Or perhaps you're a divorced single parent, overwhelmed by caring for your children and fighting a lawsuit with your ex, while holding a full-time job. Your goal is to find someone to take care of you and your problems. You marry a man willing to jump right in and deal with the chaos, including disciplining the kids. He helps with the lawsuit, but is ineffectual in other areas. Now you're angry that he's failed. Your goal is unrealistic. You can't expect an idealized person to come in and clean up all your messes. Invariably a hero falls off the pedestal.

Step 2. *Separate fact from fantasy.*

To take action, you need to assume an active role and ask questions based on real facts and information. You can't keep putting yourself in a position of blaming others when things go wrong and you've ignored warning signs.

> *Your version is:* We have a big family and our own demanding careers. The architect will take care of the house renovation and receive a 10 percent override. What a relief! What do we know about building codes, siding, and structural problems? He's the expert. He'll do a good job for us."
> *The fact is:* It's wise to take expert advice, but that's not the same thing as suspending judgment and handing someone a blank check. You need safeguards like firm cost estimates before the architect goes ahead with any portion of the job. Otherwise you risk unwelcome surprises like, "I had to redo the whole electrical system" and "The job called for it."

> *Your version is:* This broker's fees are too high, but he made money for my friend. I'll agree to them because he's a hotshot.
> *The fact is:* You're focusing on the broker. How do you know there aren't other brokers who do the same thing and charge half as much? Watch out. Shop around.

> *Your version is:* He's a wonderful, strong man who will manage the kids and my other problems. We'll lead a happy, family-centered life together.
> *The fact is:* He's a strict disciplinarian who came in like a sergeant and set limits. Yet your son still gets drunk; the other children don't listen to him. His values are also different from yours. He wants to

spend vacations and other free time alone with you, not at Disney World with the kids.

Step 3. *Recognize and remove emotional roadblocks.*

Many factors conspire to reduce your power to reason and see the truth about your appointed hero, such as:

Desperation. Understand that despair makes you vulnerable and able to think less rationally. When you feel hopeless, you grab at any lifeline. That's why you're attracted to a hero. However, your hero can't make life safe and secure for you. You need someone who will share in the struggle, not rescue you. Whether you share a little or share a lot, the issue has to be discussed in advance. Then, when there are inevitable difficulties, you've laid some groundwork.

Greed. Greed blinds you to deals that don't quite "add up." The drive to get rich quick leaves you open to moneymaking schemes you'd reject under other circumstances.

Awe. It's human nature to give up control and to let a hero take care of everything for you. After all, you're in good hands—according to him or her—and you're eager to believe it. The fact is that it doesn't matter how educated or brilliant or talented you are, there's always someone who has expertise you need and do not possess. Problems arise when the words, "Just leave it to me," are so reassuring that they play right into and fuel your *Looking for a Hero* BlindSpot. When your appointed expert becomes your hero, the temptation is to stop taking responsibility or an active role in areas that affect your quality of life.

Step 4. *Ask for feedback to inspire positive change.*

Anytime you think someone has the magic touch, stop and remind yourself, "I may not be thinking clearly." Then:

Talk to an objective observer. Someone you trust can point out any lack of due diligence on your part. If several of your colleagues tell you the CEO is using you, pay attention.

Be alert to the substance, not just the pretty pictures. When your wife or a friend advises you that, for a fraction of the price you can find a qualified CPA who values your business and will do his best to keep the tax man from your door, don't dismiss this advice. If you do, that's a signal that you are looking for a hero.

Step 5. *Act in your best interests.*

Resist seduction by the celebrity culture. Celebrity culture is a seductive element that distracts you from your goal. It's tempting to sign on with a consultant to the elite whose client list includes billionaires. If Park Avenue investment bankers think he's wonderful, who are you to argue? Because you're starstruck, you won't question anything.

Focus on the product, service, or results—not the individual. Ask, "Am I getting what I need?" When you go to someone for professional services, realize that a fancy office and impeccable haberdashery are not crucial to doing a good job. You need good medical or legal or financial advice and the attention you're paying for. You're blinded by glamour if you pick a lawyer because she wears expensive clothes and you never ask her to describe her specific approach to your problem or to demonstrate that she's had success with similar cases. Buying into the "sizzle" intimidates and gets us into painful situations.

Seriously consider people who don't have charisma. Beware of intensely negative feelings, as well as intensely positive ones. Otherwise you may miss out on valuable resources. If the doctor isn't wearing a designer suit or his office is the size of a phone booth, you may feel tempted to discount him. But these details are no guarantee of expertise. Listen and ask questions before you judge. He may be a brilliant practitioner. Don't reject people automatically.

Remember that context counts. Understand that your goal and the expert's goal may be different. For example, a surgeon's objective is to operate because that's what she does, but your goal is to get the best treatment. The two aren't necessarily the same. The goal of a salesman or a contractor is to make money for himself. If you believe your interests are his priority, you're going to be disappointed.

Recognize this person is not a god. When you find yourself hero-worshipping, realize this is just a human being with the same faults and limitations as the rest of us. Maybe you're becoming involved with the physician who cured your sick child. The doctor was always there when your son needed help, day or night. Realize, however, that the same workaholic ways that make the doctor always available to patients actually bode ill for a romantic relationship. The person may not have the time for intimacy.

Take responsibility. If you get taken in, remember, you let this happen. You believed this person because you needed someone else to take responsibility and make decisions for you. You believed the salesman because you wanted to buy that particular car. You hoped the lawyer would win your lawsuit. You trusted the doctor to have *all* the answers and didn't seek a second opinion—or you feared that he'd get angry with you if you did.

Classic Cases of *Looking for a Hero*

There is a fine line in assessing the relative roles of the deceived and the deceiver. A highly skilled con artist can fool many intelligent people. But if you factor in a glaring *Looking For a Hero* BlindSpot, then there is virtually no hope for making rational decisions.

Raymond

Raymond, a thirty-two-year-old married physician, is someone whose heart beats faster at the thought of an oil gusher. Show him a documentary on offshore rigs and he's glued to the screen. So perhaps it should come as no surprise that Raymond decided to invest in an oil well. He wanted to believe that he could triple his money, and he convinced himself that the investment was a sure thing.

Raymond mentioned to a friend that he had some cash and was looking for an investment that would generate a fast return on his money to pay off college and medical school loans. The friend invited him to a presentation about investing in oil. Raymond was immediately hooked by the beautiful offices and the sumptuous meal served before the presentation. He was impressed by the charismatic sales rep, who had a Ph.D. in economics, and the engineer, a Ph.D. in geology, who helped supervise the actual drilling. Raymond was enthralled by the whole operation.

The salesman discussed minutely detailed financial information that no one in the audience quite understood. People asked questions like, "What is the quality of the oil?" which had nothing to do with the likelihood of making money on the investment.

Suddenly a man in the back of the room questioned the fact that not a single one of the partnerships mentioned in the brochures ever earned back the original investment, let alone made a profit. The salesman brushed off the inquiry as being irrelevant, although, ironically, it was the only relevant question anyone asked all evening.

Raymond missed this red flag being waved right in front of him. He was too entranced with the idea and the glamour of the situation to notice discrepancies. It was a tremendous high when the salesman invited him on a helicopter tour of the oil fields. Raymond felt like an oil magnate. Five years later, Raymond's $35,000 investment has returned less than two thousand dollars.

Around the same time, the real-estate market softened, and Raymond and his wife had an opportunity to buy their dream home at a fantastic price. Because they'd blown their cash on the oil investment, they had to let the house go. The house has skyrocketed in value in the last five years.

Of course the fact that oil is an exciting business was of absolutely no consequence to Raymond in achieving his goal of paying off his debts. His own vulnerability to deception and another person's ability to take advantage of his BlindSpot caused him to act against his own best interests.

Melanie

You're also a prime target for a hero when you're on the rebound. If you've been dumped, you feel rejected and lonely. When someone woos you with ardor and persistence, you welcome the attention. Melanie, a twenty-eight-year-old flight attendant, found her hero when she met and became engaged to a divorced stockbroker. Her fiancé, Bill, claimed he lived with his parents, but he called her only from pay phones and repeatedly warned her not to contact *him* at home. He never invited her to meet his mother and father, and told her his two daughters lived with his ex-wife. Melanie accepted his explanations without comment. One day, after Melanie had bought her first cell phone, she received a message from Bill. His number appeared on the phone, and she returned his call—only to discover Bill's wife on the other end of the line. He was wed to (and living with) her all along.

Melanie never wondered about the strange phone arrangements and other oddities and never asked questions because she didn't want to hear answers that might force her to break her engagement. For the same reason, she never sought feedback from friends. Before meeting Bill, she had an ill-fated love affair that resulted in an unwanted pregnancy. After having the baby, she gave it up for adoption. Six months later, Bill came along. Feeling guilty, ashamed, and very alone, Melanie was thrilled with the attention Bill showered on her. He not only wanted to marry her, he came complete with a ready-made family. Melanie had thought she'd never have a husband and children of her own. She was especially susceptible to a hero because she felt out of sync with all her married friends. She didn't want to know the truth. In the long run, however, she set herself up for heartbreak.

Reclaim Your Balance

Whether you're making a major purchase, investing, or involved in other decisions, there is no connection between charisma and value. If you suspect that you're succumbing to someone's "sizzle" at the expense of good sense, say to yourself, "I'm too impressed with this guy. There's something wrong."

The same advice applies if you're swept off your feet by a beautiful, vivacious woman who introduces you to a glamorous social life and seems like the antidote to your loneliness. The trouble is, she's not the answer to your depression. *You're* the one who has to deal with that. If you convince yourself otherwise, you're going to be deeply disappointed.

Regardless of the circumstances, stop and check things out. If you feel competent and knowledgeable, you're less likely to be seduced and make a serious mistake.

CHAPTER 12

BlindSpot #6: Being a Hero or Savior

The urge to save humanity is almost always only a false-face for the urge to rule it.

—H. L. MENCKEN

TO FIND OUT IF YOU HAVE THE *Being a Hero or Savior* BLINDSPOT, rate each statement below as follows:

1 = disagree most of the time
2 = disagree some of the time
3 = agree and disagree about equally
4 = agree some of the time
5 = agree most of the time

__ I have a track record of trying to rescue or save people.
__ I regularly give advice without being asked.
__ My self-esteem is tied to helping other people.
__ I continue to try to help people even when it's become clear they don't want help.
__ I seem to be drawn to people who are self-destructive.
__ TOTAL

Your score and what it means:

20–25: *Being a Hero or Savior* is a major problem across the board.

14–19: You have some serious issues in certain areas.

8–13: Some issues need attention.

7 or less: You have little or no problem with *Being a Hero or Savior.*

Any score above 7 means you are prone to trying to be a hero or to rescuing others.

Understanding This BlindSpot

The *Being a Hero or Savior* BlindSpot—wanting to help others in order to meet your own needs as much or more than theirs—is mired in self-destructiveness. This BlindSpot explains why you're always attracted to women in trouble (or men who "need" you), why you keep incompetent employees on the payroll or loan money to deadbeats, and why you collect draining friends who are always in one crisis or another at work, at home, or in their love lives. The appeal of the opportunity to "assist" cannot be denied.

When you have this BlindSpot, you can't see that these people often don't want to help themselves or that you're hurting yourself by engaging in this behavior. If you're always bailing people out of jail and getting them jobs they can't hold onto, you disrupt your own life. Your energy is channeled away from meaningful growth activities and people who might add to your well-being. Your actions are cloaked in supposed "good deeds," which come at high cost to other more positive possibilities in your life. This BlindSpot also interferes with developing balanced relationships with people who are competent, responsible, and in charge of their lives.

The Dangers of This BlindSpot

The *Being a Hero or Savior* BlindSpot draws you into doomed emotional relationships that cause you pain. It can also bankrupt you because helping the "victims" frequently involves doling out financial aid. This BlindSpot leads to misplaced trust in the wrong people and can appear in selective areas of your life. For example, you may fall in love with abused women with a history of drugs. You can't resist helping them and don't see the danger in these relationships. You trust that they will not steal your money or possessions to feed their habit and that they will eventually be rehabilitated. Of course this never happens.

What's Behind This BlindSpot

We all enjoy being admired by others. If you're a hero or savior, however, you bask in the glow more than most and like being placed on a pedestal. Or you feel you have no value as a person unless you are helping someone else. In many cases, whether or not the other person needs or wants assistance is beside the point—as is the question of whether you are knowledgeable enough to provide effective help. Often you actually encourage the "victim's" dependency.

Maybe you chose women who have beautiful faces and figures, but virtually no self-esteem or ability to cope with the responsibilities of daily life. A few months after you plunge into a live-in relationship or even marriage, you complain that she's depressed all the time or is overspending you into bankruptcy. You vow you'll never choose such a person again, but inevitably you do. The combination of beauty and poor self-image is irresistible.

Even if you've asked friends to warn you that "you're doing it again," you ignore the warnings that you yourself requested. Often the *Being a Hero or Savior* BlindSpot works in combination with the *Wishful Thinking* BlindSpot (see chapter 7), which leads you to think, "This time will be different." You believe neither your own experience nor the experience or advice of other people.

Imagine you're a young widow. Lonely and anxious to provide your sons with a male role model, you remarry. When your husband loses his job, he asks for a loan from your late husband's insurance money to open a store. Because you want to be supportive and protect his self-esteem, you ignore the small voice within that cautions the money is family security and should not be touched. You let him talk you into signing over $40,000 of the insurance proceeds. Your new husband loses it all on a commodities market tip. For religious reasons, and because you don't want to be alone again or have your family disrupted, you remain with him and continue to lend him money for his business ideas, none of which pan out.

This BlindSpot isn't limited to your love life or friendships. Perhaps you're so enamored of being a hero to your children that you buy $200 worth of lottery tickets every week, then tell your son and daughter all about the trips around the world and cars you're going to buy for them. "It's going to happen this week—$30 million, all for us," you fantasize. In the meantime, money is always tight, and you can't buy a house because your lottery expenses take such a big chunk of your paycheck.

Maybe you focus on helping society at large, rather than individuals. You labor tirelessly for charities and other worthy causes, but your devotion saps so much of your time and energy that you have little left for your own family. You and your spouse lead separate lives. When your mate walks out one day, you're shocked. Sadly, you never saw it coming.

Key Elements of This BlindSpot

The factors that fuel the desire to be a hero or savior are:

Grandiosity

Grandiosity leads you to feel a kind of omnipotence and believe you're needed to "fix" people—or you think your love and patience will heal them. You presume you know better than they do, and you may seek needy people out. For some women, the savior role links to their traditional role as caretakers.

Or maybe you like being "a big shot." If someone you barely know asks you for a $10,000 loan for a business deal, you relish the idea of having the power to help out financially. You agree to make the loan. Then shortly after, he disappears—along with your money. You now discover he has a long record of similar scams. It never occurred to you to wonder why he came to you, a virtual stranger, to back his business venture. You didn't want to know why. Being a hero felt too good. Similar feelings lead you to overtip waiters and cab drivers.

Guilt

Guilt can contribute to savior behavior. You may have trouble firing incompetent workers. Although you warn them repeatedly about poor performance, they continue to disappoint you. You complain about them every night to your mate, yet you can't bring yourself to let them go. You like feeling that your employees need you and you don't want to be "the bad guy." You feel guilty that you will condemn them to the unemployment lines and that their families will suffer. So you give the employees another chance—and another and another. Four years later, you're still complaining and the offenders still hold the same jobs.

Overcoming *Being a Hero or Savior*

The *Being a Hero or Savior* BlindSpot can cost you a great deal financially and emotionally. To change this self-destructive behavior, lead yourself through the Foolproof Plan. The five steps help you understand why you don't see the truth about needy people until it's too late and how to resist this damaging pattern.

Step 1. *Focus on your objective.*

Know your goal, whether it's to help people, or marry someone to share a happy life with you, or run an efficient company. Don't lose sight of it. Are you achieving your objective? If not, you need to reexamine your strategy and change course.

Maybe your goal is a satisfying marriage. If you've wed several times, you obviously haven't accomplished your purpose. Is it because you invariably pick mates who are immature, helpless, or irresponsible? Then it's time to try something else. You need to admit to yourself, "These kinds of people haven't worked for me." If you want something different now, look for someone who can stand on his or her own two feet, be a full partner, and consider your needs, too.

Perhaps your goal is to run a profitable business, but it isn't happening. Is part of the problem unproductive employees? Then your approach must change. Remember, savior behavior stems from your need to be admired or needed—and that has to be examined. It's hard to do, but it's important.

Step 2. *Separate fact from fantasy.*

Take action based on real facts and information, not just your version of them. For example:

> *Your version is:* This person needs my assistance again. Of course I'll help.
> *The fact is:* People have to want to deal with their own issues. If they're not willing to solve their own problems, and you still try to help them, you are operating out of your own need to rescue. In any case, you may not be equipped to offer them help. Ask yourself whether you have the knowledge and/or experience to really make a difference in this situation.

> *Your version is:* I have to hire this person even though I know he's lazy and unreliable. He's my friend and he's been laid off. How can I employ someone else instead?
> *The fact is:* Your friend doesn't follow up on the job, shows up late for appointments, and constantly takes time off. He'll lose your customers. Commonly the people you rescue don't change, and you're left feeling disappointed.

Step 3. *Recognize and remove emotional roadblocks.*

These obstructions stop you from achieving your goals:

Self-centered reasoning. This blocks you from seeing the other person's perspective. You simply assume that someone else wants what you want. Maybe you constantly try to help people who have alcohol problems. You look at them as if they were you and ask, "What would be helpful to me?" But what's helpful to one person doesn't necessarily work for someone else.

Needing to be needed. Surrounding yourself with people who are wounded birds and can't cope with daily life indicates that you want to be a savior and feel gratified by being needed. This is very different from being a reliable friend, an effective volunteer, or a good citizen. Rescuers rarely make anything better for others and often wind up encouraging self-destructive behavior because they're always there, ready to bail the people out.

As psychotherapist Tina Tessina, Ph.D, author of *It Ends with You: Grow Up and Out of Dysfunction*, observes, "Relating to competent people takes autonomy and understanding of boundaries. You have to know where your responsibility begins and where it ends. Rescuers don't know where their responsibility ends. Dysfunctional people don't know where their responsibility begins."

Feeling you don't have a right to say no. If you've always taken care of people who have fed off you, you may feel you don't have a right to say, "I won't pay all the bills." Professional rescuers commonly come from chaotic backgrounds where both parents may have been alcoholics, substance abusers, mentally ill, or extremely immature and irresponsible. As small children, the rescuers learned to take charge. They took responsibility for paying the bills, making appointments and seeing that they were kept, and other tasks of daily life because no one else was capable of doing so. It's a habit that's hard to break.

Guilt. Feeling responsible for committing an offense is human, but it's destructive when unjustified. If your goal is a successful company, guilt that prevents you from firing people who can't perform well stops you from hiring others who will make a contribution and help everyone prosper.

Step 4. *Ask for feedback to inspire positive change.*

Feedback is a major way to get the information you need to deal with your BlindSpot. It's impossible to self-correct without it because you need discussion back and forth to help clarify what's going on. But you must be open to hearing feedback. If your friends tell you that you have "the broken wing syndrome," because you're always finding little helpless creatures and trying to "make it all better for them"—listen. If your family warns you that the woman you want to marry is "trouble"—pay attention. If you get feedback contrary to what you think, you need to talk to other sources. That's why you get second and third opinions.

Some people have an easier time getting feedback than others. If you have difficulty making up your own mind, you may seek feedback because you can't think for yourself. If you resist getting feedback at all, you may not be able to entertain the possibility you don't know what's best or right.

Step 5. *Act in your best interests.*

Differentiate savior behavior from positive help. Rushing off to help people who *repeatedly* get into trouble is different from helping someone who has had a run of bad luck. In the latter case, the person is truly a victim and deserves assistance. If most of your friends or lovers seem to be incompetent, something is wrong. Examine your own behavior. If you're always rescuing, ask yourself why you are involved with these people and what you want to accomplish. Unless it's your life's work to help people, your other relationships will suffer.

Look for better ways to feel good about yourself. Savior behavior may make you feel important, competent, and in control. But other people's neediness masks your own insecurities, so you don't have to face them. You avoid the discomfort of examining fears of inadequacy or weakness. You do pay a price. You risk being taken advantage of, although you're probably the kind of person who wouldn't dream of using someone else.

Decide your purpose. And stick to it rather than deluding yourself. If you want an interesting person in your life and know the individual is unresponsive or self-centered, that's your choice; but don't loan him or her money thinking you're necessarily going to be paid back. Don't be surprised when the person is chronically late and ignores your birthday. Ask, "Is this relationship serving my purpose?" If the purpose is to hang out with an exciting public figure, go ahead, but know what you're getting into and set limits.

A Classic Case of *Being a Hero or Savior*

The *Being a Hero or Savior* BlindSpot plays out in many ways. However, a classic case is the story of Jessica, a successful commercial photographer. Jessica met her husband Curtis at a photography gallery when she was thirty-seven and very anxious about still being single. He was a plumbing supply salesman who hated his work and wanted to become a photographer. Jessica encouraged him to build a portfolio in his spare time and get more experience.

After they became engaged, Curtis quit his job and started freelancing, without discussing it with Jessica. He made no preparation for this change and still hadn't assembled a portfolio. But he expected Jessica to support him financially while he got started. He told her, "If I have to be a salesman the rest of my life, I'll kill myself." Jessica felt angry and shocked. Friends warned her that he was using her as a meal ticket. But she married him anyway.

Throughout her life, Jessica had always taken care of people who took advantage of her help, so it never occurred to her that Curtis should contribute to the household expenses. She felt that she didn't have a right to say, "No. You need to get a job to bring in some money while you're getting started." She believed he'd work hard and be successful, but he did neither. Anytime she advised, "You've got to do this or that to get assignments," he'd threaten suicide.

The breaking point came when Jessica started having health problems and they were fighting constantly. "I had replicated my childhood," she told us. "Curtis was in a deep depression. I paid all the bills. I realized that he not only wanted me to support him, but also wanted to dump all his emotional stuff on me. I finally understood that this was not all my problem to fix." The marriage had lasted fourteen months.

The pressure of her age and biological clock was part of the reason Jessica tolerated Curtis' shortcomings and married him anyway. She also grew up with parents who fought constantly and were out of control. To keep order in her world, she became a "fixer." As an adult, she had lots of friends who needed her. She kept so busy looking at other people's lives and what they should do that she never recognized her own needs or her own best interests. Her relationship with Curtis was familiar territory and unconsciously comfortable.

A few years later, Jessica married a loving man who earned a good living. She still struggles with being a "fixer," but she is managing these issues better. She notes, "I am sometimes controlling in my present marriage, but my husband is a strong man, not a leaner. I now realize that my friends don't need me to fix them all the time. It's arrogant and presumptuous of me to think I know better than they do."

Balanced Is Best

Close relationships work optimally when there is a balance of power. Yet that is exactly what's missing when you fall into a pattern of *Being a Hero or Savior*. This is a specious way to handle your own insecurities. It does take courage to face them head on instead, but it's also the path to acting in your own best interests.

CHAPTER 13

BlindSpot #7: Overwhelming Emotion

If you're seeking revenge, you'd better dig two graves.

—OLD SAYING

TO FIND OUT IF YOU HAVE THE *Overwhelming Emotion* BLINDSPOT, rate each statement below as follows:

1 = disagree most of the time
2 = disagree some of the time
3 = agree and disagree about equally
4 = agree some of the time
5 = agree most of the time

__ I have a tendency to make quick decisions that I later regret.
__ I have invested money or purchased big-ticket items without checking references or options.
__ I have been told my anger or jealousy offends people.
__ Fear often stops me from taking important positive action.
__ My impatience has caused problems in my life.

__ TOTAL

Your score and what it means:

20–25: *Overwhelming Emotion* is a major problem.

15–19: You have serious issues in some areas.

8–14: Some issues need attention.

7 or less: You have little or no problem with *Overwhelming Emotion.*

Any score above 7 means you make decisions based on extreme emotion.

Understanding This BlindSpot

The *Overwhelming Emotion* BlindSpot—allowing intense feelings to impair your good judgment—propels you to make dumb decisions or take reckless action you would reject under ordinary circumstances. This BlindSpot explains why you repeatedly "fall in love" with disastrous business ideas (or inappropriate people), or blow up at those important to your career, or get conned by "ambulance chasers" at times of crisis—and sometimes why you cheat on your spouse.

We all experience powerful emotions, such as passion, jealousy, revenge, fear, sadness, or grief at times. These are normal human feelings. However, when one of these emotions dominates your thoughts to the point of destroying your ability to think, you're a target for trouble. You're more likely to take a course of action that will hurt you and makes no sense. For example, quitting a job on the spot because someone else got the promotion you deserve may satisfy your outrage, but it usually damages you. A new job may not be so easy to find. Other *Overwhelming Emotions* are costly, too. They separate you from the people you care about and cause you to feel rotten about yourself. The challenge is not to banish these feelings—emotions are emotions and we all have them—but to manage them, instead of letting them manage you.

The Dangers of this BlindSpot

This BlindSpot is dangerous because unbridled emotions rush you into self-destructive action. Vengeful feelings can grow so strong that they incite to violence. Jealousy run amok is a common motivation for murder. In less dramatic circumstances, jealousy can drive away the love of your life or poison what could be a gratifying relationship with a sibling.

Overwhelming fear of aging often leads to infidelity and broken marriages. Maybe your new boss is twenty years younger than you are and you're no longer the stud in bed that you used to be. You're so afraid of losing your power at work—and your virility—that you turn to another, younger woman to prove yourself. The self-deception doesn't work, of course. But fooling yourself is easier than dealing with your fear.

Even the government understands the danger of making decisions based on intense emotion. That's why federal law (and most states) require a three-day recision clause for door-to-door sales contracts. The clause recognizes that when you are approached at your home (or someplace other than the seller's usual place of business) you are likely to feel pressured to make a quick decision. To protect you, the clause allows a three-day cooling off period to change your mind for any reason at all—and cancel.

What's Behind this BlindSpot

When emotions overwhelm your reasoning processes, you actually *react*, rather than *respond* to a situation. There's a huge difference between these two behaviors.

When you *respond*, you use thought rather than impulse in making a decision. Thinking takes time, which causes a delay between what you feel and what you do about it. That time lag may be the safety factor that stops you from plunging into a calamity. You think over the decision to quit—or to buy $1,000 worth of carving knives—before acting on it.

In contrast, when you *react*, you move instantly and impulsively, without the intervention of thought. At times spontaneity is a good thing; it is essential to creativity, to a satisfying sex life, to having fun, and sometimes to safety—as in jumping out of the path of a speeding car. At other times, however, thoughtless instant action causes catastrophes.

An extreme example of this BlindSpot was seen a few years ago, when Court TV aired a case of love combined with rage. The case concerned a femme fatale on her third marriage. Unfaithful to her previous spouses, she was also cheating on her current husband, while simultaneously manipulating a besotted boyfriend. She sent letters full of lies to the boyfriend charging that her husband was physically abusing her. The boyfriend flew into a rage, shooting and killing the innocent husband, which is what the woman wanted from the very beginning. Then he turned the gun on himself. The wife did go to prison, but not before two people died. The point is, when you're too incensed to stop and reason, as this boyfriend was, you self-destruct.

Everyday life offers many less extreme examples of self-destructive paths that may not kill you, but cause harm nonetheless. For example, getting even with a coworker who has wronged you feels good at first, but revenge has a way of inflicting damage on you as well as your target. Your actions may be viewed as evidence of poor judgment and damage your professional image.

Key Elements of This BlindSpot

The *Overwhelming Emotion* BlindSpot boosts your chances of being deceived by others (or yourself) and encourages you to take irresponsible risks. This BlindSpot features various levels of:

Impulsiveness

Impulsivity becomes problematic when you can't stop yourself from taking senseless action. You become so flooded with emotion about what you want to do that you make quick decisions in order to deal with the cascade of feelings. If you're crazy about a second home, you close your eyes to important considerations like the location or the inflated price, and buy it regardless. Or you spontaneously pick up the phone to call someone who has enraged you and tell the person off or reply to an infuriating email as soon as it hits your inbox instead of taking time to calm down.

Tendency to Jump to Conclusions

Jumping to conclusions is a side effect of impulsiveness. You take assorted facts, spin them into an interpretation that may be flawed—and act on the appraisal before checking out the reality. Maybe your wife talks on the phone with her mother or her friends. When you come home from work, she doesn't hang up. It's a common reaction to conclude, "She doesn't love me." In fact, there may be many reasons for her behavior, none of them having anything to do with lack of love.

Grandiose Fantasies

Grandiose fantasies lead you to follow your dreams blindly. Dreams and goals are important. Everybody should have them. They give us hope for the future and are a vital part of a meaningful life. But something is very wrong if you're so in love with fulfilling your dream that you lose your good judgment. There's a difference between creative risk taking and irrationality. Perhaps you're a professional enthralled with the idea of owning a restaurant, and you plunge right in. Only later do you learn that the hours are horrendous and you can't take vacations. In addition, restaurants have a high failure rate and financing is a headache. It also doesn't occur to you that the skills necessary to run a successful restaurant differ substantially from those required to practice law, dentistry, or medicine. The *Wishful Thinking* BlindSpot (see chapter 7) often works hand in hand with *Overwhelming Emotion.*

Overcoming Overwhelming Emotion

Highly emotional situations invariably impair your power to reason properly and make it impossible for problem solving to take place. To stop strong feelings from working against you, follow the Foolproof Plan below. The five steps will help you analyze your behavior, anticipate situations that stir strong emotions, and stop them from triggering bad decisions.

Step 1. *Focus on your objective.*

Know your goal. Keep it front and center. Ask yourself, "Am I achieving what I want?" Suppose your goal is to make money marketing your own clever product ideas. Instead, you've lost all your money on one failure after another. If you're going to stop repeating the same mistake, you need to ask yourself, "What am I not seeing?" You must rethink your strategy.

Or perhaps you've just bought a house. Both you and your spouse are swimmers, and your goal is to build a pool—fast. Your plan: hire the contractor who promises to complete the job quickest. Is this strategy likely to achieve your objective? If your priority is speed to the exclusion of other criteria such as reliability and quality of construction, you might wind up in trouble.

Maybe you're divorced and your goal is to get married again to someone with whom you've fallen wildly in love. You want to make up for your failed first marriage and prove you can sustain a relationship. In this case, your objective must change. There are good reasons to remarry, but disproving your ex's assertion that "no one can handle you" isn't one of them. What's the rush to the altar? You need to make sure this person is right for you.

Step 2. Separate fact from fantasy.

Base your decisions on undeniable reality, not fiction. For example:

> *Your version is:* This contractor can build a pool in five months, less than half the time it will take the three other bidders on this project. That's all I need to know. I'll do whatever it takes to get my pool fast. I'm hiring him.
> *The fact is:* How can the speedy contractor deliver so much faster than everyone else? Does he have a larger crew? You need to find out what he's doing differently from the other bidders and check out his references to make sure he's reliable. You're paying lots of money upfront. You don't want to wind up with empty promises, legal hassles, and maybe no pool at all.

> *Your version is:* My spouse just died and I want to sell my house. I can't afford it now that I'm a widow (or I can't cope with caring for it now that I'm a widower).
> *The fact is:* Selling the house may be the worst thing you can do. You'll be giving up the comfort of familiar surroundings just when you need them most. The house may be largely paid for, and anything else you buy might cost you more. Don't underestimate your options and yourself. Take your time and put off this decision until you can think clearly and make more rational (not emotional) decisions.

Step 3. *Recognize and remove emotional roadblocks.*

Beware of pressing ahead with a decision due to grandiosity or other misleading roadblocks, such as:

Impatience. If you must have that condo or car right *now*, you're at risk for trouble. Yes, it's hard to wait when you really want something, but you need to take the time to conduct due diligence. Pay attention to signals that caution, "Wait a minute. Something is not right here." If you feel a faint doubt in the bottom of your stomach, don't silence it.

Jumping to conclusions. Recognize there are many valid ways to interpret behavior and your reading isn't necessarily the correct one. We can all agree on a description of someone else's behavior, but disagree about what the person *meant*.

Self-serving perceptions. Blaming your last fiasco on bad luck dooms you to repeat the same mistake. If you lost your entire investment (again) because you didn't conduct appropriate product testing and market research, it's not due to fate.

Loss. The *Overwhelming Emotion* BlindSpot is a particular threat at times of major loss, such as divorce or the death of someone important to you. Grief fogs your vision, which is why many people advise you not to make important changes for a year. You feel more fragile, less confident or able, less attractive and affluent than you really are.

Self-centered reasoning. There's something to be said for drawing on your own instincts, especially when you've been right in the past. But if you've usually been wrong, your own feelings are the worst kind of research you can rely on. You're fooling yourself if you indulge in self-talk that runs, "I'm all the market research I need. I think it's a good idea."

Step 4. *Ask for feedback to inspire positive change.*

If you're engulfed by emotion, you're literally blind to how impaired you are. You desperately need a reality check. After a loss, seek out the advice of friends and family—and your personal lawyer and accountant—before making any big decision. If an idea or business venture enthralls you, listen to friends who ask "How do you know this will fly?" and arguments that might deter you. When relatives shake their heads in disbelief and say "This is a crazy thing to do," pay attention. Following your dream is a positive thing to do, but only if it stands up to the test of reality.

Use yourself as a source of information, too. Ask "What would I advise a friend to do if he were building this pool (or opening a restaurant)?" And look at your own past experience. If your ideas haven't worked before, why will they work now?

Step 5. *Act in your best interests.*

Acknowledge the consequences of your behavior. When you have the *Overwhelming Emotion* BlindSpot, you are unable to look at the potential result of your action or decision. Are you willing to be unemployed or go bankrupt or even go to jail?

Examine the downside of any decision. It's easy to see the pluses in a course of action, but it's the disadvantages that people tend to ignore. Before writing an angry letter to a client, think it through. Do you really want to burn your bridges when you might want to work with that client in the future? Maybe you'd prefer to tear up your letter. To help yourself weigh the pros and cons, conduct a Risk Assessment Inventory (see page 59).

Slow down. When you feel strong emotion, recognize it as a warning signal to stop and wait before acting. Situations that you would have handled easily and thoughtfully when you were feeling calmer may now rile your temper or seem overwhelming. Before making a decision you may later regret, give yourself time to "sleep on it." That old bromide happens to be very good advice. Things *do* look different in the morning.

Realize that calm makes you more effective. Often you can't understand that acting overemotionally makes it less likely you'll reach your goal. If you want to talk a police officer out of a ticket, you may think that raging will intimidate him or her, but it's actually going to insure that you do pay a fine. Travel magazines tell us that if you miss your flight and rant at airline personnel behind the desk, you're usually less likely to get the alternative flight you want than if you're calm.

Identify your vulnerabilities at this time. What are the circumstances that tend to trigger overwhelming emotion for you? You need to know because powerful feelings distort your ability to absorb new information and make good judgments. Are you afraid to be alone? Insecurity about living by yourself may blind you to your best option after a failed relationship. Instead of immediately attaching yourself to someone else, you need to be able to wait to get to know the person better. Having a circle of friends you can turn to when you are lonely helps you tolerate living solo.

The need to be adored is another vulnerability that gets you into trouble. If you seek out people who are madly in love with you, you're more likely to choose needy people who aren't good for you.

Do you keep making snap decisions? Be aware that's a pattern for you and tell yourself, "Halt." When shopping for a major purchase, keep your eye on what the item is supposed to do for you and what you really need, rather than falling in love with the bells and whistles. If you're buying a new computer, it's easy to focus on features you don't even understand and won't use. If you're grieving a loss, remember there are very few decisions you have to make *now*.

Don't eliminate emotion. Fear of emotions may be as much of a BlindSpot as overwhelming emotions and may hurt you just as much. You may avoid a particular feeling, such as tenderness or love and allow others, such as anger or aggression to surface. Or you may avoid all emotion. Your philosophy is, "If you let your feelings rule, you'll make poor decisions." However, you pay a heavy price for suppressing your emotions. You can't have intimate relationships in adult life without them. If you insist on peace and calm when your lover or spouse wants to discuss a couple problem, you may respond, "You've ruined everything. Everything was fine until you brought this up." As a result, difficulties between you never get discussed. But they don't disappear. They fester and grow. You need to learn different ways to handle your emotions other than avoidance. Counseling or therapy can be helpful.

A Classic Case of *Overwhelming Emotion*

When you're impaired by the *Overwhelming Emotion* BlindSpot and the impatience it often involves, you're at risk for financial and other decisions that mess up your life. The story of Les is a case in point.

Les was married for fifteen years when he fell in love with another woman. He decided to tell his wife about the affair with Karen. His wife reacted by ordering him out of the house and immediately starting divorce proceedings.

That was okay with Les. He wanted the divorce as badly as she did. He promptly packed his bags and moved into Karen's apartment. This had been Les' way throughout his adult life. When he decided he was in love with someone new, he was always ready to scrap all remnants of the previous relationship—never mind the consequences. Now Les wanted to get his wife out of his life and marry Karen as quickly as possible. However, Les' divorce attorney took a different view of the matter.

"If you try to rush these divorce proceedings, it's going to cost you a fortune," the lawyer advised. "Your wife is taking a tough stand as it is. If her attorney senses that you're in a hurry, we will lose all our negotiating leverage. You and Karen should just live together for now and let the process play out. Once the terms of the divorce are settled, there's plenty of time to get married."

Les couldn't wait. He wanted the divorce finalized immediately, whatever the cost. "Okay, you're the boss," the frustrated lawyer responded.

"You're right about me being the boss," an irate Les answered. "It's my life we're talking about, and my choice."

Les got his quick divorce and immediately married Karen. But he lost almost everything in the financial settlement, including his house and his life savings.

Today Les admits that the lawyer was right about not rushing the negotiations. He married the woman he wanted. But they are struggling financially, and that could have been avoided if he'd been a little more patient.

Les' emotional reactions led him to significant financial losses. Like many people, he became impulsive when he got anxious. He took action as a way of dealing with the anxiety. He couldn't tolerate advice from his lawyer, which required him to slow down and think carefully about the consequences—regardless of the obvious merit of that feedback.

Becoming More Effective

When you're so traumatized or passionate or fearful that you can't think straight, you're not equipped to make important decisions. But you can learn to manage your emotions more effectively. The first step to taking better control is awareness that "I'm doing it again."

CHAPTER 14

BlindSpot #8: Bad Timing

A stone thrown at the right time is better than gold given at the wrong time.

—PERSIAN PROVERB

TO FIND OUT IF YOU HAVE THE *Bad Timing* BLINDSPOT, RATE EACH statement below as follows:

1 = disagree most of the time
2 = disagree some of the time
3 = agree and disagree about equally
4 = agree some of the time
5 = agree most of the time

__ I often bring up topics to discuss at the wrong time.
__ I too readily take reckless risks.
__ I have a history of letting windows of opportunity pass by.
__ I give up on relationships or ideas too soon—or stick with them longer than I should.
__ I have trouble adjusting my behavior to new situations.
__ TOTAL

Your score and what it means:

20–25: The *Bad Timing* BlindSpot is a major problem.

15–19: You have serious issues in some areas.

8–14: Some issues need attention.

7 or less: You have little or no problem with making timely decisions.

Any score above 7 means you suffer from poor timing.

Understanding This BlindSpot

The *Bad Timing* BlindSpot—the failure to make timely decisions—is more than just being in the wrong place at the wrong time. This BlindSpot stops you from recognizing the importance of timing in almost everything you do. It interferes with predicting accurately how events are likely to unfold—whether the new person you've met has potential as a marriage prospect, whether an investment is apt to make money, whether you're likely to get the raise you expect. You don't effectively assess the odds of a favorable outcome. As a result, you act too precipitously when caution is the prudent course—or too late or not at all, missing out on opportunity. Or you pick the wrong time to raise a potentially contentious issue with your partner or your boss, reducing the chances the person will agree to what you want. When faced with a set of circumstances, you play your hand badly.

In order to function optimally in life, you need to be able to evaluate the chances of success in any endeavor. This assessment is a crucial part of effective decision making. When you have the *Bad Timing* BlindSpot, you skip this important step. You plunge into ventures without looking ahead at potential consequences, or you pass up attractive possibilities, or stay mired in hurtful situations. Should you stay with your lover (or your job) or should you leave? Should you start a new business or bide your time? All of us face such questions in our lives. The *Bad Timing* BlindSpot increases the odds of making a poor decision. For example, you decide to hire a new bookkeeper in the middle of tax season. Yes, the old one needs to go, but is it smart to bring in someone new *now*? Or you opt to quit your job before hunting for another one, rather than looking around while you're still employed. Then you discover that many companies see you as a more attractive job candidate when you're still employed rather than when you're out of work. It also helps to collect a paycheck while you're looking.

The Dangers of This BlindSpot

This BlindSpot is dangerous because it blocks intelligent foresight. It discourages you from advancing your interests and providing for contingencies to protect yourself. When circumstances don't go the way you anticipate, *bad timing* stops you from modifying your behavior to deal with the new reality. It's important to your well-being to know when a relationship is going nowhere and when it's time to bail out and move on with your life. It's critical to recognize when the odds that a project will succeed are no longer in your favor; you need to shut it down. If you have the *Bad Timing* BlindSpot, you don't consider these options.

This is the BlindSpot that prevents you from seeing that your company is collapsing around you. You don't see signs that you're sailing on the Titanic. After all, how could a prestigious corporation go out of business? Everybody else knows it's happening—toilet paper is no longer stocked in the restrooms. Yet you're blind to the clues that all is not well and it's time to look for another job. When you're finally let go, you're shocked. If you'd networked and contacted executive placement services earlier, you'd probably have a new position lined up by now—and you wouldn't feel so victimized. The same failure to see early signs of problems and deal with them while they're still manageable leads marriages into trouble and dashes retirement plans. If you want a comfortable retirement, you have to look ahead and save and invest in your thirties and forties. Wait for your fifties, and you're apt to come up short.

What's Behind This BlindSpot

Lack of vision, the inability to take care in providing for the future and postpone gratification, stands in the way of well-timed decisions. The clearer your vision, the more likely you are to make timely choices and take advantage of openings that arise. It's vision that helps you reposition when events take an unexpected turn.

In the film *The House of Mirth*, based on an Edith Wharton novel, lack of vision destroys a life. Lily, an independent, single woman gets caught up in the narrow-mindedness of a society that leaves such women with few options. Determined to marry for love, Lily turns down the proposal of a wealthy man who can solve her growing financial problems. When her money troubles worsen, she is prepared to compromise her principles. But by then the wealthy suitor is no longer interested. As Lily's fortunes deteriorate, other opportunities for deliverance present themselves—but in each case, she is not ready to accept the inevitable compromise that's required of her. Ultimately, she becomes a woman nobody wants.

Unwillingness to compromise makes it impossible to shift gears and deal with change. It's smart to make concessions at times to get at least some of what you want. Rigidity and stubbornness are self-destructive. In Lily's case, the *Not Knowing How You Come Across* BlindSpot (see chapter 10) also played a role. She overestimated how desirable she actually was.

Key Elements of This BlindSpot

Features of the *Bad Timing* BlindSpot include:

Risk Aversion

Risk aversion inhibits you from seizing opportunities that make good sense. You're afraid to take a chance, even when the odds are stacked in your favor. For example, when a neighbor across the street offers his spacious home for sale at a bargain price, you find an excuse not to grab it, even though your family needs more room and the property offers great potential for appreciation. You reject even the best financial options. The thought of monthly mortgage payments disturbs you, or you don't trust yourself to make a good decision.

Blindness to Consequences

This BlindSpot prevents you from considering both the upside and downside of taking action at a particular time. Imagine that you're bidding for a major project and you suspect an employee is covertly passing important information to a competing company that is bidding against you. When you discuss your suspicions with your partners, you're advised to "wait and see" before confronting the individual. Instead you think, "Why bother to put it off," and you let the person go. Another key employee, the suspect's friend, soon quits, and both of them join a rival organization that proceeds to win the multimillion-dollar contract. Believing "It's simpler to go ahead and do it" achieves the very outcome you wished to avoid. If you'd timed it differently and waited until after the bidding date to act, you might have won the contract. On his own, without his friend, the employee wouldn't have done much damage.

Self-Serving Perceptions

You blame your failures on bad luck, which stops you from examining your mistakes and avoiding more of the same in the future. If you miss a great opportunity to merge with another firm, you rationalize it wasn't worth taking the chance or it wasn't such a good deal. You remain blind to what's really going on—you're immobilized by unwillingness to take a risk.

Overcoming *Bad Timing*

No one can be right all the time. But you can boost the odds of positive outcomes in your life by developing the knack for good timing. You can position yourself in a manner that invites good fortune—and assess with some degree of accuracy when it is best to take (and *not* take) action. The five-step Foolproof Plan below will show you how:

Step 1. *Focus on your objective.*

Know your goal. Don't allow yourself to be distracted. Is your goal to own your own home? Have you achieved it? If you're still renting even though you're financially able to buy, you need to rethink your plan. Passing up good deals as you wait for the perfect moment to purchase won't get you where you want to go. The ideal time may never arrive.

Perhaps your goal is a raise. If you asked for it, but didn't get it—or got a lot less than you wanted—you need to look at why you haven't achieved your objective. It's not only how you discuss a sensitive subject like money with your boss, but *when* you discuss it that makes a difference. If you made your pitch the day after he lost a promotion or his pet project was rejected, you put yourself at a disadvantage and reduced the chances of gaining his enthusiastic support.

Or maybe your goal is marriage, but you've never come close. You've had three major love affairs over the years, and each time you walked out over the first important disagreement. Now you're all alone. Either you need to change your goal and adjust to remaining single, or you have to change your tactics to get what you want.

Step 2. *Separate fact from fantasy.*

To make time-critical judgments about your life, check out the facts instead of rationalizing. Life is full of uncertainties, but you can minimize their effect with thoughtful analysis.

Your version is: I want to succeed in the fashion world, but I'm too inexperienced to assist a famous designer. I'm turning down the job offer even though it's everything I've dreamed of. I'll fall on my face.
The fact is: The offer arrived after you met the designer and showed him your work. Obviously he thinks you can do the job. It's human to feel anxious in a challenging situation, but disastrous to let lack of self-confidence and the possibility of failure distort your judgment. This is the chance of a lifetime. Stretch.

Your version is: This relationship isn't right if we're fighting about money. We should split. I'm out of here.
The fact is: The best of relationships require hard work, and disagreements come with the territory. It's a fantasy to think that other couples don't have problems at times. Learn to negotiate and work out differences instead of continuing to cut and run.

Your version is: If I buy the house, something may go wrong. What if I lose my job and can't make the mortgage payments. I'll lose everything.
The fact is: Your job is secure, and you can afford the mortgage. The price is right. Taking a chance means there is a possibility of loss. Real estate isn't always a good investment. But if you never take a chance, even when the odds are in your favor, life can be bleak.

Step 3. *Recognize and remove emotional roadblocks.*

The goal is to make thoughtful reasoned decisions rather than automatic snap judgments governed by fear or excitement. Awareness is a first step in managing these tendencies:

Fear of risk. To help yourself deal with this fear, weigh the advantages and disadvantages of a decision. Take the Risk Assessment Inventory on page 59. Also ask yourself, "What's the worst case scenario?" If your nightmare is that buying a house will lead to financial ruin, realize that you might lose some money. Prices can go down as well as up. But it is highly unlikely that a well-constructed home in a good neighborhood will be a disastrous investment.

If you take a glamorous job and can't handle it, the worst possible outcome is that you'll get fired. Even if that happens, you can get a job similar to the one you had before, and you'll have gained a great learning experience. You really don't have much to lose.

Self-serving perceptions. Instead of blaming failure on fate—or assuring yourself, "I did everything I could," when that isn't true—take responsibility for your mistakes. Admit you've made an error of judgment when you fail to see what's in front of you, blow your best option, or overplay your hand. If your first impulse is always to leave when trouble arises, you're focusing only on the negatives in a relationship. Force yourself to look at the positive reasons for staying together and weigh them carefully. Abandoning a promising relationship at the first hint of discord is just as self-destructive as clinging to a dead-end situation.

Also ask yourself, "What have I learned from this experience?" Maybe your spouse walks out. You could say, "She's a bitch," or "He's a bastard" and content yourself with blaming the other person for your failed marriage. You could insist, "There's nothing I did wrong." But if you do something different when you get over your hurt, you can become a better mate the next time around.

Step 4. *Ask for feedback to inspire positive change.*

When poor timing plagues you, you need help to judge whether your goals or actions are realistic.

Check out distorted perceptions. Are your perceptions misleading you? Objective thinking and a fresh perspective from an outside source can shed light on what's really going on. Talk to others who know you and/or are knowledgeable about the situation in order to form a more realistic picture.

If you're impatient or fear taking chances, listen extra carefully. Pay attention when your partners or friends tell you to be cautious and wait and see. Listen to your spouse or your sister when they repeatedly tell you you're missing out on opportunities. Remember that others are often more objective than you.

Step 5. *Act in your best interest.*

Impeccable timing isn't just a matter of luck, but also of thinking ahead about consequences and proceeding in a thoughtful reality-based way whenever you make a major decision. View everything you do or don't do in the context of time to minimize unpleasant surprises. You don't have a crystal ball, but you can increase the likelihood of success.

Avoid getting mired in regrets. Although it's normal to have regrets, it's not productive to keep dwelling on them. They don't help you feel any better, and constant complaining can drive people away. Everyone deserves a period of time to grieve a lost love or lost riches. At a certain point, however, you must work through what you could have done and should have done, put it to rest, and forgive yourself.

Recognize second chances. A window of opportunity may pass, and it may be too late to save a relationship with a particular person or take advantage of a certain investment, but there will always be other people and other opportunities. However, you do need to recognize and change patterns that have hurt you in the past.

Maybe you've made work a priority for much of your life, without thinking, "Wait a minute. Am I missing out on experiences that are really important to me?" Then a close friend dies, triggering a reexamination of your own life. It helps to evaluate priorities at such time. When you receive an invitation to an event, ask, "Are these people important to me?" and "Is this an important occasion?" If the answers are yes, the next question is, "What am I willing to give up to go?" In order to attend a friend's fiftieth birthday party, you may choose to work late the week before (or after)—and sleep less. When the people are less close, you may decide to send regrets and a gift. Setting goals and priorities keep you on track. You do have choices.

Know when to leave. It's time to bail out of a relationship or job or project when the costs of staying surpass the benefits. If you're miserable with someone far more often than you are happy (which is in the eye of the beholder) or the advantages of starting your own business outweigh the risks of leaving your company, it's time to go. On the other hand, recognize that your decision might add up differently a few years from now. Know what's most important to you at the given time.

Identify turning points. Recognize that the *Bad Timing* BlindSpot commonly appears at junctures in life when new situations demand new behaviors. If you win a big promotion, you can't follow the same old patterns now that you have added responsibility and a different role with former coworkers. Your work is more challenging and may require a whole new set of skills, including negotiating new political and social relationships. You may have to assume authority over people who used to be your peers. Now that you have become more successful, you may become the target of envy; former supporters may become adversaries. Acknowledge these changes and adjust to protect yourself.

When the kids leave home, beware of unrealistic expectations that your relationship with your spouse will flourish without new attention. Adapt your behavior to support your marriage. The empty nest syndrome signals that you are entering a new time in your life. This is a point when a refocus on the marriage takes place. It's important to renegotiate your relationship with your mate now that you're less involved in active parenting. Working together on being a couple again helps head off trouble.

Wait for the right time. Poor timing creates problems in daily life in many small, but significant ways. Discussions with your spouse about important topics such as children, work, or money are more likely to be fruitful if you schedule them carefully, making allowances for personal habits and biological rhythms. Talk to your spouse about moving to a larger apartment before morning coffee and you may be setting yourself up for a negative response. Some of us never want to discuss anything important at the breakfast table. Others need time to change clothes and relax after work. Sometimes the best time to talk is on the weekend. The point is to maximize the chances of getting what you want (and avoid unnecessary fights) with wise timing.

A Classic Case of *Bad Timing*

The *Bad Timing* BlindSpot plays out in any number of ways and situations. Just one classic example is the story of Kurt and Marsha, spouses who were unprepared for the marital adjustments that occur in retirement. At this time in a marriage, a couple's differences can destabilize the relationship. Men and women often have very different work trajectories. Men may be ready to retire, while their wives, who started working later, may be at the peak of their careers—or have important interests they want to continue to pursue.

Kurt was an entrepreneur who made enough money to live out his dream—retirement at fifty, with lots of time for travel. He and his wife, Marsha, who had stayed home to bring up the kids, decided to move to Vermont, where they bought an antique bookshop.

Marsha discovered that she loved the new business, and she took it very seriously. She enjoyed selling, talking to customers, and buying books. To Kurt, however, the store was a hobby. He wanted to travel; Marsha didn't want to leave the store for more than a week. In the course of therapy, it became apparent that the meaning of work was different for each. Kurt had achieved his work goals; Marsha had not. She thought he'd share her enthusiasm for the store, and he thought she would welcome retirement. However, like many married couples, they had never discussed their assumptions with each other.

We explained that each of them was unaware of how the other felt about the balance between travel and running a business, and that timing was an important factor in their dispute. They needed to negotiate their differences in three steps.

First, they had to clarify their expectations. Kurt wanted the bookstore to be mainly a hobby, one that would not interfere with travel plans. Marsha found it fulfilling to work actively in the business and wanted to grow the store.

Then, they had to remove value judgments from their discussions and stop blaming each other. Kurt charged, "How can you be so selfish refusing to take long trips with me after I've worked so hard to support you and the kids all these years?" Marsha counterattacked, "You're so self-centered. I stayed home for the children and now it's my turn to see what I can accomplish at the store." Such dialogue only fueled fights and stifled problem solving.

Finally, they had to compromise. Over time, we helped them work out concessions that both of them could live with. Marsha agreed to more travel after recognizing how important it was to Kurt. He became more involved in the bookstore and more willing to negotiate the length of trips. In the end, both were able to get *some* of what they wanted.

Make Your Own Luck

There's always an excuse for why others succeed and you don't. It's "He made all that money because of luck." Or, "I don't have the talent that she does." But most people have more power than they think. The knack for good timing is good judgment about your own interests. Identify ways you can either be self-defeating or self-enhancing. Watch out for damaging behavior, but also give yourself credit for what you're able to accomplish.

Part III

Moving Ahead

CHAPTER 15

Strategies for Changing Problem Behavior Patterns

The air is full of our cries
But habit is a great deadened.
—SAMUEL BECKETT

YOU NOW KNOW HOW TO UNDERSTAND WHAT YOU ARE DOING, recognize your BlindSpots, and stop them from holding you back. This is an important beginning, but there is more to do to get what you want as often as possible. To some degree, we all have behavior patterns that work against us—which are triggered by BlindSpots. Changing these patterns will help you use the Foolproof Plan more effectively. We've mentioned some of these behavior patterns in previous chapters, such as overestimating your capabilities or ignoring signs of real trouble in your marriage or a new romance. There are many more. Although we can't discuss them all, we are going to examine some common ones and show you how to modify them.

Five Strategies for Change

Behavior patterns are habits, recurrent and often unconscious ways of conducting ourselves. Because habits are ingrained in us, they aren't easy to change. These strategies will help you break free of the BlindSpots, which activate damaging behavior patterns:

1. *Notice your own destructive patterns.*

   Monitor yourself and improve your self-check skills. Practice stepping outside of yourself and observing your interactions as if you were a third party watching a videotape. What are you doing? What is the other person doing? What would an observer think about what is happening? Answering these questions helps you see your behavior more objectively. As you practice the Foolproof process in your life, you'll find stepping back and observing yourself becomes easier and easier to do. Listen, too, when someone close to you warns, "You're doing it again."

2. *Examine the part you play.*

   Acknowledge your contribution to destructive patterns, whether it's making provocative comments that invite retaliation or running away from conflict instead of working it through. You have to first admit your part in the problem before you can understand and change your responses. If you dig in your heels and get defensive when events don't turn out as you'd anticipated, you fuel your pattern. Statements like "There's nothing I did wrong" or "I was just being honest" do *nothing* to help you change your behavior in the future.

3. *Don't consider yourself a victim.*

   Even if the situation is only partially your fault, you do have to ask yourself, "What could I have done differently?" It's never productive to think of yourself as a victim, unless you were literally helpless in a situation. The victim self-image stops you from thinking of ways to change your strategy.

4. *Start thinking and behaving differently.*

   You need to change your perception of what is going on and reframe (i.e. reconceive the situation in an entirely different way and give new meaning to it). Look for exceptions to your pattern in order to gain the new perspective needed to make a change. For example, although you may not overestimate your abilities all the time—you may overestimate them under certain circumstances. If you are aware of that fact, you will then be able to think more realistically. Such insights help you turn your experience into a learning event and change your actions to your benefit.

5. *Set up a positive environment to support your goal.*

   Respect how difficult it can be to change behavior patterns and notice times when you may backslide. Based on what you've learned about exceptions to your pattern, seek out situations where you can do well. In some cases, this may involve moving into another division at your company, changing the people you hang around with, joining a support group, or otherwise modifying your environment to keep yourself on track.

   If you're struggling with a weight problem, find a "diet buddy" who encourages weight-loss behavior. Don't stock the freezer with ice cream and rationalize that you need a supply in case company comes. Don't hang around with people who regularly overeat and tempt you to do the same. Sign up for Overeaters Anonymous.

   It's crucial to remember that choices always exist. Never feel trapped. Look around for options. Don't assume they're not there just because they aren't obvious at first. Look deeper —they are there. You just don't see them.

Modifying Destructive Behavior Patterns

Below are some common problem behavior patterns we encounter in our practice. Do any of them get you into trouble in your social, family or work life? The analyses that follow will help you break out of them. When you see the mistakes you are making—as well as what you are doing *right*—you can then do more of what works and less of what's destructive. You can also see more clearly how your own behavior distracts you from reaching your goal and getting what you want.

Behavior pattern: *You argue with authority*

Perhaps you've held several different jobs, and the outcome is always the same. Time after time, when you reach a certain level, you seem to get into an argument with the boss. Then you leave. You rationalize: "The boss is a tyrant." In fact, some bosses are overbearing; every boss is not. The problem—and the role you play—may be that you have trouble coping with authority. You may not realize the damage it's doing to you, and that it's not in your interest to alienate someone who can either help or hurt you. The *Overwhelming Emotion* BlindSpot (see chapter 13) and the *Not Knowing How You Come Across* BlindSpot (see chapter 10) are at work.

To modify your behavior, look for exceptions to your pattern. For example, do you find that although you usually fight with supervisors, there's one boss you get along well with? Figure out what it is about him that makes you feel comfortable. Maybe it's a really simple thing like the fact he always smiles warmly when he sees you and asks about your kids. That puts your pattern of balking at authority in context. You realize that you get along well with that type of supervisor and that you are capable of acting in a different way. Armed with that information, you can place yourself in more of these advantageous situations whenever possible. The next time you interview for a job or apply for a transfer, you can look for a "warm and fuzzy" boss who doesn't trigger the harmful pattern of arguing, and avoid people who are cold authoritarians. This is a way to set up an environment that supports you.

The same general problem of balking at authority may arise with friends and relatives. Perhaps the arguing behavior surfaces at family gatherings. There's a fight with your brother-in-law every Thanksgiving because he tells you how to run your business or what car to buy. This pattern suggests that you may play an important part in the squabbles that constantly arise. Maybe you just can't resist making snide remarks. Ask yourself, "How can I think and act differently?" Remember: A BlindSpot is an emotional obstruction, which is influenced by how you interpret what you perceive.

You need to reframe and change your perception that "He's telling me what to do. Therefore he's a dictator." Look at alternative ways to explain his behavior. He's not trying to control you—he's trying to enhance his own self-esteem. Or perhaps he admires you and is trying to impress you—or is showing his concern and attempting to be caring. These explanations change the whole meaning of what he is doing and short circuit your anger. If you think his motive is to care, not control, you feel differently about him. In fact, most behaviors are more ambiguous than they seem. An "unfriendly" faculty member may turn out to be shy. A hostile hotel concierge may have just lost her father. Her behavior may have nothing at all to do with you.

Behavior pattern: *You can't relate to competent people*

Perhaps you tend to get along with needy friends, yet have trouble relating to people who function well in life. This pattern suggests that you have the *Being a Hero or Savior* BlindSpot (see chapter 12). The part you play is you're comfortable only when you're in a one-up position, which reflects low self-esteem. Deep down you feel, "I'm not really worthy of well-functioning friends who succeed in life." So you pick people who are always in one crisis or another and need you. You avoid people who are your equals (or superior in some ways and have something to teach you) because you feel intimidated and you think you don't measure up. You're threatened by your fear of looking stupid or incompetent in comparison.

How can you think and act differently? What's the worst that can happen if this person thinks you're dumb or incompetent? Do you fear being ridiculed? That's unlikely to happen because you probably have a lot more going for you than you take credit for. But even if someone asks, "How stupid can you be?"—so what? You write the person off your list. But if you won't take the risk, you miss out on stimulating, enriching relationships. The better your self-esteem, the easier it is to risk people thinking poorly of you. Fear of humiliation is a human feeling, but it reflects self-doubt and is something to overcome.

Behavior pattern: *You can't hold onto friends*

Do you find that your friendships turn over every three years, rather than evolve, change, and last. This pattern suggests that you have unrealistic expectations about what friends are supposed to do for each other, and you wind up being disappointed. The part you play is thinking you deserve unlimited, unconditional attention and support from your friends, regardless of the circumstances, when in fact your demands are often unreasonable. If you expect a friend to drive you to the airport at 4:00 A.M., when you can take (and can afford to take) a taxi, the problem is *you*. You've got the *Wishful Thinking* BlindSpot (see chapter 7) and the *Not Knowing How You Come Across* BlindSpot (see chapter 10). Just because you'd do it for your friend, you can't expect she would do it for you. Self-centered reasoning stops you from looking at your friend's point of view. This is not an emergency, and she has to be clear-eyed for a morning meeting.

Or maybe you attend a performance by a friend who is a professional violinist. At the end of the show you go backstage to see him, but instead of congratulating him and discussing the enthusiastic audience response, you talk for ten minutes about the merits of various composers. The friend who is naturally excited after performing and wants to share his elation, feels ignored and disappointed. Your contribution is lack of empathy for the person. You appear arrogant, uncaring, and blind to the needs of your friend. You are acting from the *Not Knowing How You Come Across* BlindSpot (see chapter 10). Figure out how to act differently. Ask yourself, "If I was the one up on stage giving a great performance, what would I want my friend to say to me afterward?" This question forces you to think in a different way.

Look at the turnover in your friendships, realize you're doing something wrong, and change your behavior. You may be unaware that you distance people by acting competitive, snobbish, or overbearing. You turn off people because you're hostile and think, "All people are rotten." You need to modify your thinking and change your behavior.

Realize, too, that relationships change throughout life and some turnover is to be expected. Friendships may wax and wane because one of you moves or gets married or divorced or has a baby or changes jobs and you no longer work in the same office. Things change, you change, you have different lifestyles and interests and less in common.

Behavior pattern: *You lose your temper easily*

Uncontrolled anger is a factor in *Overwhelming Emotion, Bad Timing,* and other BlindSpots, causing both personal and professional damage, and hurting relationships. Maybe you get so angry so fast when you and your wife have a fight that you are unable to talk about the issue at hand. The whole discussion then centers on your yelling at her rather than on the issue you're mad about. The reality is if you're going to have a serious discussion, your spouse needs to trust that you won't explode at her. If you blow up, she either feels intimidated or the encounter becomes so highly emotional that no problem solving can take place. The part you play is feeling flooded by emotion and that your behavior is justified. You think that you have a right to react this way.

Or perhaps you're too quick to be offended and verbally attack anyone who slights you. If someone is five minutes late for an appointment, you become vicious. Your behavior isolates you because people put up with such behavior for only so long. Being quick to lose your temper means you're more out of control than you realize. Here again you feel self-righteous.

A surgeon we knew got himself in serious trouble for throwing instruments around the operating room. The nurses tolerated it because he was so talented, until one of them finally reported him to the hospital administration. Although the surgeon was threatened with the loss of his medical license, he defensively insisted, "I only get angry when I feel that my patient is not getting the best care."

If losing your temper is your pattern, you need to modify your behavior. Feeling anger doesn't have to lead to acting on it. The first principle of anger management programs is to learn how not to automatically react to a provocation from another person. "If someone pushes your buttons and you automatically retaliate," participants are told, "you are admitting that you can't control your buttons. You might have to leave the room to take control, rather than throw a punch." If you can't control your verbal outbursts you might have to do the same thing.

You don't need an anger management class to recognize how harmful uncontrolled rage is for relationships and to avoid minimizing it. People who lose their tempers frequently are blind to how anger is building in them and how this mounting rage affects other people. They will say that their anger rises from 0 to 100 in a split second, but that isn't true. There is always a little warning beforehand, whether it's a knot in your stomach or a tightening in your head or shoulder. The anger management approach teaches ways to recognize the stages people pass through and effective actions to take before losing control and erupting. For tips on anger management techniques, check anger management websites online or read a book on the subject.

Behavior pattern: *You nag*

Perhaps you want your partner to adopt a healthier lifestyle. You nag him or her to exercise and lose weight, which is your pattern any time you want a change in behavior. However, your partner resents being told what to do, becomes even more stubborn, and the two of you wind up fighting. Nothing changes. The *Not Knowing When You're In or Out of Control* (see chapter 8) and the *Not Knowing How You Come Across* (see chapter 10) BlindSpots are at work here.

The dictionary defines nagging as a persistent way to torment another person with irritating complaints or fault-finding. Like many people, you don't understand that nagging is ineffective communication and causes unnecessary friction in a marriage. Your contribution is you feel powerless, that you aren't being heard, and you don't know of any other way to get your message across. You don't realize that nagging usually doesn't work. It only aggravates both partners.

When you say, "I'm concerned that you don't get enough exercise," you're expressing worry about your partner's health. Nagging is a way to express your concern. The trouble is, if the person still refuses to exercise and ignores you, you become increasingly frustrated. You continue to nag—and get the opposite result from the one you want. You need a different approach. You might try, "I'm asking you to exercise over and over again, and it probably sounds like nagging. But I'm very worried about your health. Do you want me to keep reminding you? Or do my reminders turn you off?" If your partner replies, "They do turn me off," that may be hard to accept. Yet you then have the chance to discuss whether there is anything else you can say or do that will influence him or her positively. It's quite possible that your goal is impossible to achieve and you must surrender and accept that. The person has to want to change.

Maybe you also nag because your partner drops clothes on the floor when undressing. Because you want him or her to pick them up rather than leave them there, you say, "I can't stand it when you throw your underwear all over the place." The person might mumble, "What a nag. What's the big deal about dropping my clothes?" In this case, he or she doesn't understand the reason you're so upset. Instead of nagging, it's far more effective to say, "When you leave your underwear on the floor for me to pick up, it makes me feel like your mother, not your partner. And that infuriates me."

This statement opens the door to another, more productive kind of discussion. It explains that you're not putting a value judgment on what the person is doing and saying, "My way is better." It describes what's important to you, rather than blame or attack. Then the individual might respond, "I have to be so careful at work, I don't want to have to worry at home, too." Both of you express personal preferences and use "I" statements, which are much less threatening than "you" statements such as, "You're a slob."

Behavior pattern: *You withdraw*

The flip side of the nagger is a withdrawing individual. Your contribution is you ignore the other person, fueling feelings of helplessness and creating animosity. This leads to even more nagging. Try an alternative way of behaving. If your partner nags about messiness, make a direct statement like, "I think what you're asking is unreasonable" or "I think you're much too fussy in the way you want the house. It makes me feel I can't relax in my own home. I don't care if it's a little messy." Such comments are far more effective than withdrawing and can open negotiations between you. The other person may counter, "Well, I think it's unfair," and a discussion begins.

Both of you need to realize how you are affecting the other. Hopefully it will become clear that there isn't a particular right or wrong. There is a neat person and a less neat person—and this is an issue that the pair has to work out, ushering in the age-old conflict about whose standards should prevail.

Behavior pattern: *You can't say no*

The ability to set limits in relationships is crucial to your autonomy and self-esteem. Yet you may feel powerless to negotiate when asked to do something you don't want to do or to accept something you feel is unfair. As a result, you're always putting your own needs last. You have the *Not Knowing When You're In or Out of Control* BlindSpot (see chapter 8). Your contribution to your pattern is you may urgently want to be liked or fear others will be angry with you. Or you don't want to be perceived as uncooperative, uncaring, or stingy.

But you can't assure that someone will like you by giving in to all his or her requests. If you always say yes, you wind up trapped into attending events or doing favors you really don't want to do. In the process, you probably simmer with resentment. You need to change your perception of the consequences of turning someone down. You may fear losing a friend by refusing his request for a loan, but it's rare that a person ends a relationship because you refuse one favor.

If you always say yes due to fear of authority, figure out alternative ways to respond tactfully and diplomatically. For example, you might reply to an intimidating husband, "It's hard for me to talk about your cousin's party because I'm afraid that if I say I don't want to go, you'll bark at me." Reframe the perception that you can't stand up to him and that you're helpless. Change your self-talk to, "I can stand up" and ask yourself, "What's the worst thing that can happen?" Another effective question is, "What would I do if I wasn't afraid?" The answer may be that you'd say, "Your cousin is always rude to me, and I don't like him. Go to the party without me."

Behavior pattern: *You can't speak up and assert yourself*

Your contribution is passivity. The *Believing in Myths* (see chapter 9) and the *Not Knowing When You're In or Out of Control* (see chapter 8) BlindSpots are at work here. The key questions are "What's going on? What would it take for you to be more assertive?" Are you frightened by the prospect of conflict and competition if you speak your mind? Not everyone is prepared to handle such issues. For many women, being assertive means being seen as "pushy" or "a bitch." Only you can decide what's more important—being liked or getting what you want. But you do have a choice.

In relationships, every time you speak up you risk conflict or tension. First you must decide what is most important to you. What is your goal? If your goal is to advance in your career, is it more important to you to assert yourself and get promoted—or be liked by your coworkers? In education the goal is to learn something. Yet many girls don't speak up in class because they feel it's unfeminine. When you have a question, you have to ask it if learning is primary.

Behavior pattern: *Cheating on your spouse, thinking it won't affect your marriage*

It's common to think you can control an adulterous affair—that your spouse will never know and your marriage won't be affected. This tunnel vision blinds you to the big picture. Even if your spouse doesn't find out, an affair drains the marital relationship because intimacy is now shared among three people. If you're upset about something, you will confide it to your lover instead of your mate. Often your spouse does find out. You may even unconsciously leave clues to make sure that happens.

Clarify what you want. Some people want both a mistress and a wife, and lead successful second lives. But if you want intimacy in your marriage, don't fool yourself that you can have it when you engage in an affair.

It's very important to analyze your behavior patterns for yourself because then you can examine what you did correctly (and incorrectly) and decide how you can change outcomes in the future. When behavior patterns are close to the surface of your awareness, they're relatively easy to modify. If you don't see the pattern even when you're told about it, however, you need professional help. See chapter 17 for further information.

CHAPTER 16

Using Feedback to Control BlindSpots

You will find that the truth is often unpopular and the contest between agreeable fancy and disagreeable fact is unequal.

—ADLAI STEVENSON

IMAGINE IF YOU COULD PREDICT THE FUTURE! THERE WOULD BE NO relationships that end badly, no financial or business moves that go sour. The timing of your decisions would always be impeccable, and you'd be able to size up accurately every situation and every person who crossed your path. Unfortunately, no one has a crystal ball. But by now you've learned a great deal about the eight critical BlindSpots and how to eliminate or minimize their potential for self-damage. With a little extra light (that is, a bit more information) you can further increase your ability to control your future. The right kind of feedback from the right people illuminates BlindSpots. It provides information you might not have considered before and can radically change the outcome of events. Be aware that feedback can come from friends, family, peers, colleagues and coworkers, and hired professionals. The point is to recognize when you need help and seek it, be open to it when it is offered, and be able to use it to your advantage.

The story of Nicole illustrates what we mean. Nicole was a professor of economics who wanted to move into the business world. She couldn't understand why she was having difficulty landing a corporate position for which she was highly qualified. After a number of unsuccessful interviews with male personnel officers, Nicole was beginning to take these rejections to heart. Then she reached out to a friend, who referred her to an executive placement consultant.

The consultant was impressed with Nicole's qualifications. He suggested that they role-play an interview from beginning to end. After this exercise, the consultant concluded that Nicole needed to make three key changes. "When men interview a qualified woman for an executive position," he noted, "they tend to pay special attention to her handshake. Your handshake needs to be a lot more firm. You also need to increase eye contact and update your wardrobe."

What Nicole didn't realize was that she had to project a different image for a different arena. Although her clothes weren't an issue in academia, they sent the wrong message in the competitive corporate world. In that environment, she needed to come across as someone who was confident, in charge, and looked the part. Her presentation had to change in a new venue that involved different expectations and required increased visibility. Fair or not, the concept of dressing for success *is* based on reality. Although wardrobe may not matter in some settings, such as a research laboratory, it means a great deal in many others.

Nicole was skeptical that such superficial changes would make a difference, but she figured that she had nothing to lose by trying them. She turned to a fashion-savvy friend for advice on buying some new suits, shoes, and adding smart accessories to complete the new look. She practiced firming up her handshake to convey confidence and looking people in the eye to show her interest and indicate that she was listening attentively. After implementing these changes on interviews, Nicole received a job offer within a month.

Obviously, this woman's success involved more than a new look and a stronger grip. But if she hadn't been willing to ask for and listen to feedback, she might still be blind to how she came across. She'd still be unaware of how she needed to change her strategy to achieve her goal.

Unfortunately, there are psychological barriers and other factors that block you from gathering and processing feedback. You must be alert to them in order to get where you want to go.

Resist the Resistance to Ask for Help

Whether you're worried about a shaky romantic relationship, a child falling behind in school, or buying into a new business, you want hard facts that will help you make constructive decisions. It may seem obvious that a major way to tell what the facts are is to ask others. Yet many of us hesitate to turn to someone else for help for a variety of reasons:

You believe asking for help implies weakness or ignorance. Seeking assistance requires you to admit that you may not have all the answers or do not know what to do. You surrender a measure of control to someone else and allow yourself to be vulnerable. Revealing that vulnerability may be very difficult for you. When struggling with work-related problems, for example, it's reasonable to seek information from knowledgeable, trustworthy people in your organization or industry. Instead, however, your first impulse under stress may be to defend yourself and tell everyone what a great job you're doing. The show of bravado is actually a way to mask your weaknesses. As a result, you never seek the help or get the data you need to change your strategy.

In our personal lives, as well as in business, many of us never even consider asking others, "What can I do to make friends? I've moved to another state and don't know anybody?" or "How can I get along better with my mother-in-law?" Before we ask such questions, we must be willing to admit that there's a problem that we can't cope with. Ironically, the act of surrendering and making the admission can be a tremendously freeing experience that opens doors to many possibilities.

You don't know what you don't know. It's common to delude yourself, "I can run a successful corporation, so of course I know what is best for my married children." Business and personal relationships are different fields of knowledge and require different talents.

Success in one area doesn't necessarily translate into success in another, and might even be a negative influence. Drive, decisiveness, and ability to take charge is part of your career success, but these qualities work against you if you try to dictate to your thirty-two-year-old son. A plumber may have the knack for relationships while a brain surgeon may not. The reality is, you can't know everything.

Some people who don't know what they don't know actually cause a lot of trouble in the business world. They interfere in matters where they shouldn't, getting in the way. Others may not want to work with them.

You're stubborn. It's a universal joke that male drivers have difficulty asking for directions. They'd rather drive around totally lost than stop at a gas station for help. They feel that they're somehow diminished as people if they must ask others for assistance. On the other hand, women typically have a different BlindSpot. Many refuse to play politics and build alliances in the workplace. These strategies plug you into inside information that helps advance your career and alert you to impending developments. Political savvy and networks are what it takes to climb to the top in most careers.

You're a perfectionist. It's been said that perfection is the enemy of good. This may sound like a contradiction, but it is not. Perfectionism perpetuates BlindSpots because it keeps you so focused on what's going on internally—the need to be flawless—that you lose sight of larger issues. For example, perfectionists often have trouble meeting deadlines because, for them, the job is never totally finished. They can't let go and don't realize that others become angry with them because their projects are late.

The reality is, no one ever has the entire picture. You're always working with partial information, and there's nothing wrong with that. What's important is to know when you have *enough* data to proceed. You should not be so distrustful and insecure that you can't move. If you wait to get every last scrap of information, it may be too late to make a good decision. The opportunity may have passed you by.

Perfectionism also stops you from delegating. You think that no one can ever do the job as well as you can.

You don't want to hear bad news. Market research requires a certain amount of humility because you're saying, "I may want to jump and develop this product, yet I don't have all the answers. I've got to ask other people what they think, and the danger is I may not like what I hear. But I'm going to have to listen." That doesn't mean you have to accept every opinion. But you have to be open-minded enough to hear what you don't want to hear, which may require you to cancel your plans or modify them.

Sometimes it's hubris—arrogance stemming from excessive pride—that makes you deaf to feedback. The ancient Greeks knew all about the sin of hubris, which still hurts people today. Ellen was a patient of ours, who was offered a large, lucrative project for her consulting firm. She called up an industry colleague who had handled the client in the past. "Why aren't you working with him anymore?" she inquired. The colleague replied, "Because he's impossible. He keeps changing his mind and he's always screaming. He was giving me a nervous breakdown. Turn it down."

Thrilled at obtaining such a prestigious project, Ellen scoffed at the warning. "I'm different," she thought. "I'm more of a 'people person' than Joe. I'm persuasive, and I can get along with anyone. What happened to him will never happen to me."

Ellen proceeded to learn a painful lesson. She told us, "It was a disaster. The client was never available, What's more, he didn't know what he wanted, and he was obnoxious. He also misled me about how much cooperation I could expect from his people. I finally had to pull out after wasting an enormous amount of time and effort," she says.

In this situation, Ellen started out acting prudently. She sought feedback to help herself make a good decision. But she dismissed the information she received. She decided that she was special; the facts didn't apply to her. The *Not Knowing When You're In or Out of Control* BlindSpot (see chapter 8) led her astray. Similar refusal to hear bad news has destroyed some of the most powerful companies (and governments) in the world.

Opening Up

Hiding important facts from others also does damage. When you conceal information, you block access to data that is necessary for good decision making—and you usually get hurt, as well. There is always confusion on some level. Secrets in families such as a suicide, homosexuality, adoption, abortion, or even artificial insemination, impact on everyone. The information is kept hidden out of shame or fear, but there are almost always negative consequences. The secret injects undercurrents into a relationship that the other person senses but doesn't know how to interpret. One way or another, trouble eventually bubbles to the surface.

Maybe you're a married man who fathers an illegitimate child while serving abroad in the military—and you remain in contact with the secret family. Even if your children only learn of the deception after your death, they're likely to have mixed emotions: some joy and anger at finding a sibling and confused feelings about the betrayal of their mother.

Keeping secrets also imposes enormous burdens on you, especially if the secrets are supported by lies and deceptions. For example, it's not uncommon to exaggerate qualifications when looking for a job, such as claiming that you have supervised many more people than is actually the case. Or your résumé may contain outright lies in an attempt to hide your lack of credentials. You may describe yourself as a college graduate when you are not. You may rationalize, "I can do a good job. What difference does it make if I don't have a piece of paper?" But don't underestimate the effect of withholding information. There is always a price to pay, even if it's in terms of how you feel about yourself for fooling other people. Eventually, most frauds are unmasked at great personal cost.

One of our patients, the owner of a successful nursery and garden supply center, told all her friends and relatives that she graduated from the University of Colorado. In fact, she actually dropped out at the end of the freshman year. Someone else told a similar story when she applied for a teaching position.

In the business owner's case, there would be no career-damaging consequences if she were found out, although she would certainly be embarrassed. People might view her differently and wonder about her veracity in other situations. But the teacher knew she could be ruined. Both individuals told us that they felt guilty, fraudulent, and continually afraid they'd be discovered. "I'd start sweating every time a conversation came around to the topic of college," says the owner of the nursery.

In an extreme case, the chairman of the board of a well-known corporation fooled himself that he could hide his criminal history. Decades earlier, he had served prison terms for armed robbery, a bit of background information that he had neglected to disclose when he joined the company—which was, ironically, a manufacturer of firearms.[1] He was forced to resign when newspaper headlines announced that he was a convicted serial bank robber.

It might be appropriate to keep some secrets, such as an old affair or a recent one-night stand, when confessing them might only do more harm than good. For example, we knew of one salesman who had long planned a trip to the Caribbean with his wife to celebrate their twentieth anniversary. A few days before departure, his employer informed him that the business had been sold and he was out of a job. Devastated, he confided the news to his brother, but he kept it a secret from his wife. She had anticipated this vacation for two years, and he didn't want to spoil it for her. It was only after they returned that he told her the truth.

Philosophers and ethics experts continue to argue whether keeping secrets in a family can be justified. It's a complex issue with no black-and-white answers. However, it is important to recognize that keeping secrets usually will have consequences. The wife on the anniversary trip felt contradictory emotions. She appreciated her husband's concern for her, but also felt angry that he had concealed such key news. Spouses do depend on unconscious contracts with each other such as agreeing to share important information.

---

1. *Wall Street Journal*, March 8, 2004.

Breaking Down Defense Mechanisms

Another obstacle to getting the information we need involves defense mechanisms, which are normal ingrained processes the psyche uses to protect itself from anxiety. These mechanisms are the unconscious means we employ to help us navigate through threats or conflict and deal with our deepest anxieties and fears. Defense mechanisms develop in early childhood, are common to all human beings, and are completely normal. However, exaggerated or rigid defense mechanisms can trigger BlindSpots.

There are many different types of defense mechanisms—and their patterns in any given individual often define his or her personality. For example, how do you handle fear of terrorism? Have you always coped with threats by avoiding them, like walking a block out of your way to avoid a bully on your way to school? Then you might unconsciously apply the same mechanism of avoidance in adult life and stay away from crowded public places that could be targets.

Someone else may cope with the same fear of terrorism in a totally different way, using the defense mechanism of anger. His motto is, "The best defense is a good offense." He may say, "We're going to get those bastards, and I'm going to support this country in rounding up suspects. I'm roaring mad." He handles any threat or conflict by getting angry.

Or perhaps you utilize a counterphobic defense mechanism, which means that you handle fears and threats by flying in the face of them. If you are afraid of heights, you may skydive or take up mountain climbing to prove to yourself that you are not afraid.

Defense mechanisms are neither right nor wrong. Each of us automatically and unconsciously deals with threats or conflicts with a particular set of defenses that are automatic and part of our personality. The problem is, all defense mechanisms are double-edged swords. The upside is they defend you from anxiety that could immobilize you, and they make you feel more secure. The downside is, when your defense mechanisms are too rigidly applied or too pervasive, they discourage problem solving, close off other options, and have the potential to blind you to the reasons for your behavior. It is then that they result in BlindSpots.

To protect yourself, the goal is to be aware of the characteristic ways in which you respond to threats. Then you can figure out how to become more flexible in your behavior during times of stress.

Keeping Calm

If you are someone who automatically uses anger to handle conflicts, you are in danger of developing the *Overwhelming Emotion* BlindSpot (see chapter 13) and the *Not Knowing How You Come Across* BlindSpot (see chapter 10).

Pete, thirty-nine, feels threatened when he thinks his wife is spending too much money. He visualizes himself going bankrupt—and then explodes. One day he called us in a panic because his wife, who is usually very tolerant, said she couldn't take his behavior any longer. We suggested that he adopt a new approach. We explained to Pete that he automatically reacted to dangerous situations with anger, the way his parents had. It was a learned response.

When Pete's wife shopped, he also experienced a danger—going broke. But here his angry reaction was *too* automatic and triggered too easily. We explained, the key word is "automatic." It means you're not in control and you're not thinking the situation through. To avoid reacting blindly, you have to say to yourself, "Whenever I feel threatened, I get angry. Sometimes the anger is appropriate and can work for me; sometimes it isn't, and it gets me into trouble." You want to figure out which situations are appropriate to express anger and which ones aren't.

Confronting Conflict

If you're an avoider, you might develop the *Wishful Thinking* BlindSpot (see chapter 7) or the *Not Knowing When You're In or Out of Control* BlindSpot (see chapter 8), in which you avoid facing and dealing with important issues. You rationalize, "Of course I won't take airplanes. They could be hijacked." But refusal to fly may impede your social or business life. People use all kinds of rationalizations for their behavior, failing to see how their fears limit their possibilities.

Learning to Ask for and Use Feedback

Difficulty in obtaining, digesting, and acting on important information helps fuel BlindSpots. Here's how to break that cycle and polish your feedback skills.

Find Out What Stops You From Getting Help

Be aware of your own personal psychological blocks. Do you hesitate to ask for information because you worry that you'll look stupid or weak? Successful people who take control of their lives know that they can only learn from their mistakes if they are willing to admit, "This relationship (or project or job search) isn't going very well." Then they ask someone else, "What steps can I take to make it run smoother?" If you don't ask, you can't find out because people don't normally volunteer such information.

Do you fear rejection or a negative response when you request help? Ask yourself, "So what if John says no? What is the worst thing that can happen? Can I live with that?" If you worry about imposing on others by asking for help, remember that most people like to be helpful. In any event, it's for them, not you, to set limits for themselves.

If impulsiveness is a problem, you may only seek information that supports what you want to do. You use this tactic because you're invested in taking immediate action and tend to ignore facts that would slow you down or deter you from your course, however disastrous. To guard against impulsive behavior, understand the difference between defensiveness (emotional resistance that indicates a BlindSpot is kicking in)—and disagreement, which is an intellectual reaction and argument.

Try to get in touch with feelings of resistance to what someone is trying to tell you. Remember that when you act defensively, you feel upset and threatened, are unable to hear the other person, and are likely to use the words *yes, but*. . . . "Yes, but" is just another way of saying no to a suggestion.

Even if we ask for constructive criticism, we sometimes have trouble hearing it. At a book-signing party, an eager author spoke to an agent he had just met about a book idea he wanted to pursue. He described the project in detail and asked for her opinion. The agent suggested several ways to sharpen the focus and make the book more timely and saleable. The author was so enamored of his own strategy that he was unable to hear what she was saying. "Yes, but . . ." he constantly replied. The agent supplied the kind of publishing advice that money can't buy, but he couldn't process it.

Factor In Your Instincts

You do need to listen to those feelings in your gut. Many successful people report with delight that they were told when they first started that their ideas would never work. But they persisted and proved everyone wrong.

Yet it's important to be realistic about your own track record. Are your instincts and judgment usually on target? You rarely hear tales about warnings that were ignored and the disasters that followed. If you're impulsive, you need to *really* listen to naysayers and see if you can pick apart their arguments (or not).

Choose the Right Sources

Not everyone's feedback is valid. You can't get good information unless you approach appropriate people and know whom to trust. Try the Source Evaluation Quiz in chapter 6 to assess the level of knowledge, self-interest, and veracity of an information source.

Use Active Listening As a Tool

For many of us, the natural tendency is to talk, not to listen. Active listening is an interpersonal skill that teases out helpful information, and lets the other person know that you hear and understand what is being said. This technique also helps you identify your own behaviors that are objectionable to others.

Active listening takes practice, but it's well worth the effort. Here's how to do it right:

- Concentrate on fully absorbing what the individual is saying. Speak only when you need to ask a question to clarify a point. Give the person enough time to say what is on his or her mind.
- Paraphrase what the person has said to ensure that you've heard correctly and understood. For example, maybe you just had an argument with your spouse. Try saying: "You tell me that I don't remember to consult you when deciding where to go on vacation and how much to spend. You say that I make you feel irrelevant and ignored when I make the decision unilaterally." Or, "You tell me that when I raise my voice and say I don't like the way you manage the money, you feel attacked." Then the other person feels heard, even if there's still disagreement.

Active listening allows you to identify what you're doing that annoys the other person—and acknowledge how your behavior makes the person feel. This information is invaluable because it opens the door to change. Once you pinpoint the offending behavior, you can take steps to modify it if you want to.

Note that this technique is different from mimicking, as in: "So you think I'm criticizing you (or impatient with you)." The difference is important. Mimicking does acknowledge what the other person has said, but it omits the crucial element of understanding the message.

Argue the Other Person's Position

This is another technique that sometimes works when you get stuck.

Switch to your mate's point of view and argue it skillfully and convincingly to let him or her know you understand the thinking. Attorneys learn to do this in law school. Suppose your spouse wants to move into the city and you want to stay in the suburbs. Your dialogue might run: "As I understand it, the reason you want to move to the city is you want to be close to the cultural life, you don't want to commute anymore, and you're tired of keeping up the house."

Consider Brainstorming

Brainstorming is a way to get a more comprehensive picture of the problematic person or situation. Brainstorming with others challenges your thinking in ways that aren't possible when you're alone. Possibilities and options will come up that you hadn't really thought about.

Technically, no idea should be off limits. The strategy is to state any idea that comes to mind without censoring yourself at first. Later on you can eliminate ideas that are blatantly unfeasible. In a typical scenario, a spouse considering taking a new job in another state asks for a family discussion of the pluses and minuses that would affect everyone's life. Family members offer ideas and input. For example, the downside for the children attending a new school is that they'd have to leave their friends. The upside is the new school has a better reputation.

Illumination Improves Thinking

Have you ever stood outside at dawn, when it's virtually impossible to see anything? In a matter of seconds, the sky becomes just a little brighter and suddenly the accuracy of your vision improves. You may still not be able to see things as clearly as in the full light of midday, but the smallest increase in light is often all it takes to improve the clarity of your thinking. Proper feedback provides that extra bit of light.

CHAPTER 17

When You Need Professional Help

Change your thoughts and you change your world.

—Norman Vincent Peale

Most of us can manage our BlindSpots with a combination of motivation, awareness, and the strategies for change already presented. Sometimes, however, a self-help book is not enough. Certain underlying disorders may make it impossible to deal with your BlindSpots on your own. Or other issues may block meaningful change and require professional help. In all of these cases there is a common denominator: for one reason or another, you don't have the strength to help yourself.

Depression

Depression is a serious mental illness that alters your thinking, mood, and behavior in ways that impair your ability to function. If you're chronically depressed and haven't the energy to make positive changes, you can't manage your BlindSpots without professional help.

Optimists see the world through rose-colored spectacles. When you're depressed, you view life through dark glasses. The world seems bleak and hopeless; an overwhelming pessimism pervades your life. TV correspondent Mike Wallace called his depression "endless darkness."

Depression is quite different from feeling "blue" for a few days. When you're merely under the weather, you retreat for a brief time, then feel better and return to normal activities. In contrast, untreated depression can last for months, years, or more.

Signs of depression include:

- Persistent feelings of sadness or emptiness
- Anxiety
- Insomnia or too much sleep
- Weight gain or loss of appetite
- Loss of pleasure or interest in activities you used to enjoy, such as food, sex, hobbies.
- Loss of energy; fatigue
- Difficulty concentrating
- Irritability
- Crying spells
- Suicidal thoughts
- Hopelessness and despair

If several of these symptoms persist for more than two weeks or interfere with your work or family life, seek professional help. Because depression feeds on itself and often worsens without treatment, diagnostic evaluation and treatment is essential.

Getting Help

Approximately 9.5 percent of the population eighteen and older (18.8 million adult Americans) suffer from a depressive disorder, according to the National Institute of Mental Health (NIMH). Fortunately, depression is highly treatable. A variety of psychotherapies and antidepressant medications are extremely effective. Appropriate treatment depends on the individual case.

The resources below, suggested by NIMH, offer referral, diagnosis, and/or treatment services:

- Family doctor
- Mental health specialists such as psychiatrists (M.D.s), psychologists (Ph.D.s), social workers (MSWs or Ph.D.s), or mental health counselors.
- HMOs
- Community mental health centers
- Hospital psychiatry departments and outpatient clinics
- University or medical school–affiliated programs
- Family service, social agencies, or clergy
- Private clinics and facilities
- Employee assistance programs
- Local medical and/or psychiatric societies

Or ask your gynecologist, or a friend you trust, for a referral to therapy or counseling. You can also check the Yellow Pages for resources under "mental health," "health," "social services," "suicide prevention," "hotlines," "crisis intervention services," "hospitals," and "physicians."

For more complete information on depression and its various forms, such as major depression, dysthymia, and bipolar disorder (manic depression), visit the National Institute of Mental Health website at: *www.nimh.nih.gov*

Chronic Anxiety

Anxiety, that unpleasant emotional state we're all familiar with, consists of psychophysiological responses to anticipating unreal or imagined danger. If you're chronically anxious, you can't calm yourself down or regulate your emotions—and cannot control your BlindSpots.

Signs of anxiety may include:

- Restlessness
- Difficulty concentrating
- Irritability
- Muscle tension
- Difficulty falling or staying asleep
- Ruminating or obsessing
- Unrealistic fears
- Pounding heart
- Sweating
- Shaking
- Shortness of breath
- Dizziness
- Chills
- Butterflies in stomach
- Thoughts you can't get out of your head (obsessions)
- Irresistible impulses to perform repetitive acts (compulsions)
- Unrealistic fears
- Feelings of panic

Because untreated anxiety can worsen and disable you, see your family physician for evaluation if symptoms last for more than a few weeks. Anxiety disorders are generally treated with medication and specific types of psychotherapy.

As a supplement to professional medical care, self-help groups and talks with a trusted friend or clergyperson may be helpful.

For detailed information on anxiety disorders, including generalized anxiety, panic disorder, phobias, and obsessive compulsive disorder (OCD), see the NIMH website (page 195).

Alcohol or Other Addictions

Addictions stop you from thinking things through. If you have a substance-abuse problem, you're in no condition to control your BlindSpots.

Alcohol

Alcohol is legal—and in moderation, it's perfectly acceptable. But millions of people have a problem with alcohol. If you're among them, your drinking problem may be a BlindSpot you're not aware of. When you drink, your intellectual functioning is totally impaired.

One way to gauge whether you can handle alcohol is to take the CAGE test:

C (cutting down): Have you ever thought about cutting down on drinking?

A (annoyed): Do you ever become annoyed when someone criticizes your drinking?

G (guilty): Do you feel guilty about drinking?

E (eye opener): Do you need a drink first thing in morning?

Most normal drinkers do not worry about cutting down and don't feel guilty or defensive about the comments of others. Only alcoholics start the day by drinking in order to fight a hangover and prevent the symptoms of withdrawal. A "yes" to even one of the above questions raises a red flag, so see your family doctor or seek out a self-help group such as Alcoholics Anonymous (AA): *www.alcoholics-anonymous.org*. This website offers referrals to AA groups and information on the program. Local AA offices are often listed in the telephone book.

Note that drinking and all other addictive behaviors involve enormous denial. If you point out to someone that he or she is drinking too much, the person often replies, "I only have three beers." Someone addicted to gambling says, "I'm not addicted; I enjoy it. I can control it." But you can't control addictive behaviors when you're in denial.

Drugs

Drugs raise different issues from alcohol because drugs are illegal. You risk severe penalties if you're caught using illegal substances, even if you only use them occasionally. The habitual drug user's behaviors are similar to those of the alcoholic, especially denial. Seek help if friends or family tell you they're concerned about your drug use.

For further information on treatment for alcohol or drug abuse, contact:

The National Drug and Alcohol Treatment Referral Routing Service:
1-800-662-HELP. Offers treatment information and referrals in your state.

National Institute on Drug Abuse and Alcoholism (NIAA):
301-443-3860. Offers free information materials.

National Council on Alcoholism and Drug Dependence (NCADD):
1-800-NCA-CALL. Information on local treatment and educational materials.

12-Step Groups

For most addictive problems, the best approach is usually a 12-step group. These groups are all modeled after Alcoholics Anonymous (AA), which has a long track record of fellowship and sufferers helping other sufferers. The twelve steps are extremely effective in combating denial and accepting the part you play in the problem. Best of all, AA groups are free and available in every part of the country.

The enormous success of Alcoholics Anonymous has given rise to 12-step groups for a variety of chemical and nonchemical dependencies. Chemical dependencies include addiction to alcohol (AA), drugs (Narcotics Anonymous), or food (Overeaters Anonymous). Nonchemical dependencies include addiction to such things as gambling (Gamblers Anonymous), spending (Debtors Anonymous), or sex (Sexaholics Anonymous).

There are also 12-step groups for families and friends of addicted people:

- Al-Anon: for spouses and family of current alcoholics
- Alateen: for adolescent children of current alcoholics
- ACOA (Adult Children of Alcoholics): for adult children who seek help for their own personality problems, even if the alcoholic parent is long dead or no longer active in his or her addiction.

Physical or Emotional Abuse

Approximately 4 million American women are abused by a partner every year. If you're a victim, you're usually so beaten down that you don't have the emotional strength to help yourself. Assistance is available from a number of domestic violence organizations and support groups. Resources include:

National Victim Center:
1-800-FYI-CALL
National Coalition Against Domestic Violence:
303-839-1852
National Domestic Violence Hotline:
1-800-799-SAFE. Offers crisis intervention and referrals

Difficulty Making Changes

Perhaps you're using this book and following its guidelines, yet the strategies do not work for you. You can't settle on a career or your marriage isn't working or you can't find a girl or a guy, no matter what you do. Then you need more than a book—you need professional help.

It's hard to change; we're built to resist it. Your BlindSpot may be too firmly entrenched to deal with on your own, or your defense mechanisms are too rigid or pervasive. Or dealing with a BlindSpot requires a strength that is not one of your assets. For example, if you can't handle your child's rebellious behavior or other problems, you need expert assistance.

Or maybe you're unreasonably jealous of your spouse. You misinterpret and misperceive his or her actions and convince yourself that your mate is unfaithful. Then you constantly check underwear, the odometer, and call your spouse at the office six times a day to snoop. Marriage requires a certain degree of trust, but sometimes jealousy feeds on itself and is almost delusional. Without professional help, it's hard to eliminate the misperception.

Feedback from Friends and Family

People who care for you often see things that you cannot. If they don't have an agenda of their own—they come from different segments of your life—and they all tell you the same thing, pay attention. Perhaps your wife insists you're too self-involved and unavailable, and your brother tells you the same thing. You need to hear that message. If you can't, this may be the time to seek professional help, which will force you to confront your behavior, rather than rationalize it away.

CHAPTER 18

Building on Success

As for the future, your task is not
to foresee, but to enable it.
—ANTOINE DE SAINT-EXUPÉRY

YOU'VE NOW READ ALL ABOUT BLINDSPOTS AND HOW TO TAKE CONTROL of them. We've seen many people turn their lives around by making more positive choices and achieving change. Here's how some of these individuals were able to recognize BlindSpots that hurt them and take effective action to stop damaging behavior. We know it's not easy to accomplish, but read on and see how much of a change overcoming a particular BlindSpot can make in the quality of someone's life

Insight into Action

For Neil, thirty-six, a rising executive in the food industry, it was a conversation with a partner in a search firm that identified his *Not Knowing How You Come Across* BlindSpot and served as a wakeup call. In the course of discussing career goals and possibilities, Neil was told, "You project a smart, capable image, but you're a screamer." The assessment rocked Neil's confidence. "I was shocked that the world saw me that way. Yet I always knew that I had an underlying impulsivity. I had made two secretaries cry at my office. One left because I yelled at her."

Neil was determined to become an industry leader and knew he had to change his image to accomplish that objective. His experience in market research had taught him about the importance of perceptions. As a result, he was able to translate his newfound insight about himself directly into action. "You have to make adjustments in a product to make it more acceptable to the consumer. If the product is wrapped badly, it had better be wrapped differently. If people don't love the taste, you'd better change it. That goes for people, too," he explains.

Neil began to observe other industry leaders, especially CEOs, and how they conducted themselves. As he noticed their body language, he became aware of his own tendency to appear tense rather than relaxed. He realized that people would look at him at times and recoil as if he had been angry with them. He could see their eyes widen. "I realized that if you see a person look fearful or intimidated, you have to try to lighten up to counter that. My facial expression conveys tension, which makes others tense. So I consciously started to smile more. I could see people relax when I did that."

As Neil moved on to higher positions at other companies, he continued to learn from role models and use his authority to create a positive work environment. He discovered that simple gestures like a pat on the back make a huge difference in motivating people. "If I walked into a sales meeting smiling, and shook hands with everyone, it changed the whole tenor of the meeting," Neil recalls.

He noticed that his voice counted, too. "Your tone is magnified when you deal with people reporting to you. Even a small note of displeasure is intimidating to someone whose job is dependent on making you happy. I realized I had to modulate my voice," he says.

He learned that a cocktail party is an occasion to loosen up, not hold tense discussions. "I used to go into a room, and if I had four problems to solve, I'd automatically go look for the people involved to talk to them about it. This was not good leadership."

Neil had to work hard on the significant changes he made, and still has to remind himself to resist cornering the first person he sees at a social event. "I also know that any executive with a tendency to be volatile must realize he can 'lose it.' Since I tend to express anger impulsively, I work to keep it down," he says.

Neil's honesty with himself can't be overestimated. This strength allowed him to immediately focus on problem solving—and create change.

Taking Responsibility for Your Actions

To break out of a destructive pattern, it's essential to look at yourself and avoid getting defensive, rather than blame someone else. Brad, an optometrist, vividly remembers the girl he pushed out of his life thirty years ago. "I was in a new relationship with a lovely, lively young woman, and I would take the bus to pick her up and take her to a movie. We both still lived at home. Our relationship was great—until she did something that offended me," he explains.

Brad's girlfriend was very possessive about her car and wouldn't let anyone else drive it, including Brad. In Brad's old-fashioned sense of masculinity, the man was supposed to do the driving. An elevated sense of pride caused him to overreact. They argued heatedly. In the days and weeks that followed, instead of seeking a solution, Brad sulked. He stubbornly waited for her to call and apologize for hurting his feelings. "Certainly I could, and should have found some way of raising the topic and discussing it with her. But I did nothing," he remembers. His goal was a deepening relationship with the girl, yet he never asked himself, "What is the result of my behavior. Am I getting what I want?" She didn't call, and the relationship ended.

Losing her, and the reasons for losing her, made a lasting impact on him. "I still recall waiting for her to call me, and the pain of not being with her. It was self-inflicted punishment—for nothing," says Brad.

This instance was not the only time Brad had cut someone off because he was angry or offended. But this incident sticks in his memory because of the sheer disparity between cause and result. Eventually, he began to understand that venting his anger provided a little immediate emotional release, but always hurt him over the long term. "That realization hit home. Since then, I have learned that there are better ways of handling disputes and disappointments. If I lose my temper nowadays (and it rarely happens), I consider it *my* failure. Life has been much smoother and richer since that epiphany."

Rather than sugarcoat his own role, Brad faced up to his actions and confronted his BlindSpot. He changed his behavior, instead of continuing a pattern that kept him from getting what he wanted and reassured him that he was right. But he still remains vigilant. A few years ago, he became upset with the young adult son of a friend and yelled at him. Mortified at his own eruption, he apologized instantly. The young man stubbornly refused to accept the apology and withdrew angrily. "It was much like my own behavior when I was younger," Brad mused. "But there was a much better ending. We made up after a few weeks."

Becoming Your Own Advocate

The belief that she had no control kept a patient named Delores stuck in a company where her considerable skills were devalued. Delores was a bookkeeper and general office manager who initiated money-saving changes and other important efficiencies. She often worked weekends without extra compensation. Yet her accomplishments were never appreciated, and she was always overlooked at raise time. Her boss sometimes ridiculed her. Afraid to take a risk and explore outside options, Delores stayed stuck in her thankless job—until a relative of the company owner needed work, and Delores was replaced.

Being fired was traumatic, and it took time for Delores to absorb the shock. Supported by friends and family, however, she gradually began to look for another job. She realized that she'd always excelled at and enjoyed computer work, and she focused her job search on the information services industry. She landed a challenging position at twice her old salary. "This worked out a hundred times better for me," she says. "Getting fired was the best thing that ever happened."

Delores was a woman with tremendous talent and ability, who had been underutilized and undervalued by her employer. Because she didn't appreciate herself, she felt helpless to be her own advocate and change the situation. But she had far more control over her work environment than she realized—and she has used that knowledge productively at her present job. She has become far more vocal about her accomplishments and lets her boss know where her strengths lie. Her newfound assertiveness has already paid off in large raises and two promotions.

Accepting and Living with Limitations

Sometimes the challenge is not to take action, but simply to accept the fact that you have no control. Victor, a Detroit business owner and the father of three sons, convinced himself that he could determine the course of his children's lives. He believed that by offering the right encouragement and opportunities, he could steer his sons to success.

"From the earliest years, I thought my kids would go to Harvard or Stanford if I just let them know the high expectations I had for them and always made sure they did their homework and studied for exams. I thought achievement and everything else would fall into place."

But Victor's oldest son failed to cooperate. "He'd come home and tell me the good news first—"I got ninety-five on the test." Then he'd hand me his report card full of C's. He was bright, but he wasn't a student." Instead of studying, he preferred to tinker with engines,and could usually be found with his head bent under the hood of a car. "He knew we wanted him to go to college, but he had other ideas. We fought a lot about it, but I learned that you can't just dictate to a child what you want him to be." Today Victor's son is an automobile mechanic and loves his work.

Victor shakes his head and observes, "It's been a humbling

experience. I know now that my son has to live his own dreams, not mine. Most important, we no longer fight the way we used to. Little by little, we've forged a close relationship."

Another patient, Maria, chose to accept the limitations of a disappointing marriage. A forty-year-old homemaker, Maria was unhappy about how her husband, Manny, the manager of a construction business, felt about spending time with her. After eighteen years of marriage, Manny was totally uninterested in Maria's company beyond an occasional dinner once or twice a month. They rarely had sex. He spent many weekends at a second home in the country where he hunted and pursued his passion for carpentry. To his credit, he was an excellent father to their three children, and the family often went on camping vacations together. He enjoyed visiting both his and Maria's parents. But he never seemed to have time to spend alone with Maria.

At Maria's insistence, the couple started marriage therapy. After the initial sessions, it became apparent that Manny had to be told, "If you want your marriage to improve, you have to spend some time with your wife." When we confronted him with that statement, he replied, "I work hard all week, and I go to the country to unwind. Our marriage is as good as it's going to get."

Maria came to recognize that although Manny was very dedicated to her in his way, he was no longer attracted to her, and he didn't want to change. It's very painful to be in a relationship where you aren't desired. Manny had no interest in other women. He had much more passion for his work and hobbies than for sex. Maria faced the fact that she had two choices: She could leave the marriage or she could find some way to stay and still feel good about herself. She was adamant about staying. She and Manny came from large, close Latino families. They saw a great deal of all their relatives on both sides. Manny treated her kindly and was very generous financially. They had pleasurable family time together.

Although Maria could not make Manny desire her, she could control most other aspects of her life. Her children would be going to college in the next few years, and she began to think about other ways to spend satisfying time. One day she very casually brought into a therapy session an elegant hand-knit sweater that she had made in her spare time. Knitting had been a passion of hers for years, and she had a talent for creating intricate patterns in exquisite colors.

In the course of therapy, Maria began to believe that her talent was a major asset. Over time, she started selling her sweaters to major department stores, and she began a work life that didn't involve Manny. Her business success not only increased her self-confidence, it also expanded her social life. In the past, her women friends had been the wives of her husband's friends, and they got together only as couples. But she now began an independent social life with women she met through her business. Maria's stimulating new circle has helped her gain a sense of herself, despite the limitations of her marriage.

Thinking Differently

Jerry, a freelance speechwriter, met Samantha at a friend's Fourth of July barbecue. He was immediately taken with the pretty, vivacious blonde who shared his passion for jazz. Over the next six months, Jerry and Samantha were inseparable. They went to clubs and concerts, got to know each other, and fell in love. Samantha, however, had a disturbing background. Her father was alcoholic and her brother was in and out of jail. Her rejecting mother regularly told Samantha, "You should never have been born." As a troubled adolescent, Samantha was sent away to a school for "difficult" children whose families couldn't manage them.

This history not only didn't cause Jerry concern, it added to Samantha's appeal. He wanted to marry her, certain that he could save her. Jerry's parents and his sisters pleaded with him to reconsider. "She's volatile and possessive, and she'll ruin your life," they warned him. He was undeterred.

Jerry had a classic rescue fantasy that he could protect Samantha from her troubled past. "I knew she had serious emotional problems, but I felt sort of omnipotent. I thought I could make her well. With my love and patience she would heal," he explains.

His rude awakening began a few hours after the wedding. On their way to a honeymoon in Canada, the couple stopped at a motel where Samantha provoked a vicious fight. Screaming, she threw lamps at him and assaulted him with her fists. The tantrum continued for days. In one town Jerry considered putting her on a plane and annulling the marriage. Yet he clung to his fantasy of saving her. "She's just immature," he told himself.

Samantha's tantrums became regular occurrences. Living with her became a roller coaster ride. Before the marriage, she seemed to love music but now hated it. She refused to go to jazz clubs, and she forbade Jerry to go. Without provocation, she became very jealous.

Jerry told us, "She thought I had an affair with every female who called me on business. I wish it were true. I'd be a legend." By then they had three sons. He rationalized, "What was I going to do? I couldn't leave them with her. I would have had to be the custodial parent. I felt they were too young for that," says Jerry.

Years later, it was a family move to a larger house that became the catalyst for divorce. Due to a glitch in school transfers, for a period of time Samantha stayed in the old house with one son during the week; Jerry lived in the new house two hours away with the other boys. They were all together only on weekends. "It was an astonishing revelation. I found out what life was like without her," says Jerry. "I felt this enormous sense of freedom from tyranny and oppression. I decided the children, then nine, ten, and twelve, were old enough for me to take custody. I wanted out." He had stayed in the marriage for thirteen years.

"I wish I had greater maturity at the beginning. Based on nothing at all, I believed that I had the ability to save her, and I convinced myself that I loved her. In retrospect I'm not so sure it was love as much as pity. And in some ways, I must have been dependent on her or I would have left earlier," he says.

For a year after the divorce, Jerry dated only musicians because music was his passion. He began to realize that he wanted something different. He found it in his current wife, who is exactly the opposite of the women he'd always been drawn to. "She fulfills my personality, my outlook on life, everything. She has a generosity of spirit, compassion, understanding, and a total willingness to try new things. She wasn't a music lover when we met, but she was willing to go with me to concerts and found she liked jazz. She's the greatest humanist I know. I did learn from my mistake," says Jerry.

Play to Your Strengths

The people we've just described all have something in common. By themselves or with the help of others, they were able to identify damaging patterns, change them, and improve their personal or work lives. Another way to function optimally is to play to your strengths.

You may have strengths that you've never considered assets. For example, you may be an excellent support person, but underestimate the value of playing a supporting role. We once attended a college preparation night for one of our children, where the admissions officer for a university spoke to this issue. "People talk only about leaders, but we're looking to gather a community," he said. "Everyone doesn't have to be president of the student body or captain of the debating team. We need people who can participate, follow, join, and often that's not valued enough."

Maybe you're someone who felt bad about yourself when you were in college because you couldn't produce a list of accomplishments. You weren't chosen for the crew team or elected a class officer. You weren't the star of the drama club. Fortunately, your mother pointed out to you that you had other reasons to feel proud. You were a wonderful audience and made an important contribution in that way. Where would musicians, dancers, and actors be if enthusiastic concert- and theatergoers didn't show up to appreciate their performances? How would our political life function without all the volunteers who lick envelopes and knock on doors to get out the vote? You not only attended all the school plays, you also worked diligently selling ads for the yearbook. You never realized that you were participating in the larger community and that you were making a contribution in your own way.

Or perhaps you and your wife have successfully engineered a role reversal. You're the full-time caretaker for your three young children; your wife is a high-octane investment banker. You're not good at initiating, but if you're told what to do you can follow through on calling up other parents to make play dates. You can be a homemaker and do the supermarket shopping. Your wife is far more energetic and assertive than you are. Both of you know where your strengths lie, respect and support each other's assets, and have a strong marriage—even though the role reversal often causes tension.

It's just as important to be aware of circumstances where you don't shine and to avoid diving into them automatically. Often we're thoughtlessly drawn to situations where we aren't at our best, setting ourselves up to perform poorly and feel like failures. A union official we know has finally faced the reality that he is a terrible committee member. "I'm often asked to join committees, so I do," he says. "But the truth is I really like to do things myself. When I have to work with others I wind up not only being unhelpful, but actually disruptive, because I get bored." Boredom may cause you to start looking for trouble and court danger instead of figuring out why you feel bored and what you can do about it. This man now acknowledges that he doesn't belong on committees. He says no to serving on them whenever possible.

The importance of staying on track with your best skills is illustrated in the classic book *The Peter Principle,* which deals with the phenomenon of people promoted beyond their level of competence in the business world. A first-rate carpenter for a construction company may advance to supervisor or to sales manager. Yet he may perform these jobs badly because totally different skills are required. Carpentry involves craftsmanship. Managing a sales staff takes the ability to deal with people and market issues.

When advancement takes you far away from your best skills, you can start fooling yourself. Ultimately grandiosity kicks in, and positive feedback from subordinates (which is often hypocritical) causes you to start believing that you are really good at these jobs. It's common, if you're a smart person, to think you can do everything well You must realize you can be smart in one area and dumb in another.

Of course, there are situations where you have to (or want to) engage in activities where you have limited talent—and that's fine as long as you don't fool yourself about it. You do have to challenge yourself at times and use your weaker skills. The key is a realistic approach. By all means take a course in math or a foreign language, even though you're not good at these subjects. Accept a challenge on the job that you aren't sure you can manage. At the same time, realize that you may have to work harder than others because this is not an area of strength.

If you're starting a business, and sales (rather than management) is your forte, you may have to bring in a manager to provide oversight. When you decide to speak at a professional conference to raise your visibility, you need to prepare more thoroughly and practice longer if you are not eloquent, and perhaps even consider a class in public speaking to improve your technique.

Success Has Many Guises—Be Flexible

It may mean neutralizing the power of a quality that works against you, or following a course you never considered before or growing the confidence to take (or pass up) a risk. Sometimes it's a matter of switching your goal to find satisfaction in life. Whatever the path that's right for you, you can achieve positive change.

CHAPTER 19

The Future Is Yours

Change is the process by which
the future invades our lives.
—ALVIN TOFFLER

YOU'VE LEARNED A GREAT DEAL ABOUT HOW TO AVOID REPEATING THE mistakes that hurt you in the past. Maybe you've even begun to think differently and take small steps toward changing your behavior. Now it's helpful to assess your progress—and learn how to keep moving in a positive direction.

How Far Have You Come?

To gauge how far you've advanced since you first began this book, retake the BlindSpot Inventory you completed in chapter 2. If you've read BlindSpots over a period of several weeks or more, take the followup inventory now. If you read the book more quickly, wait at least a month to give yourself time to digest what you've learned and start to act on it. Ask yourself the following questions again:

FOLLOWUP BLINDSPOT INVENTORY

Instructions: Using a 5-point scale, rate each statement as follows:

1 = disagree most of the time
2 = disagree some of the time
3 = agree and disagree about equally
4 = agree some of the time
5 = agree most of the time

__ My decisions usually have the outcome I anticipate.

__ When a situation doesn't work out, I can see the gaps in how I sized it up.

__ I am usually able to avoid being overcome by strong emotions such as love or fear that distort my judgment.

__ I am pretty good at recognizing whom to trust—and whom not to trust.

__ I understand what I want from people.

__ I am good at perceiving what other people want from me.

__ The messages I transmit to others are received by others as I intended.

__ My sense of timing in terms of when (and when not) to act is right on the money.

__ I take responsibility for my shortcomings and mistakes, and I expect others to do likewise.

__ I feel I am in control of my own destiny, though I'm aware that certain things are outside my control.

Compare your present answers with your earlier responses. Do you feel a greater sense of confidence about dealing with your BlindSpots? Which of the eight critical BlindSpots remain areas of vulnerability for you? Check them:

BlindSpot #1. *Wishful Thinking*
BlindSpot #2. *Not Knowing When You're In or Out of Control*
BlindSpot #3. *Believing in Myths*

BlindSpot #4. *Not Knowing How You Come Across*
BlindSpot #5. *Looking for a Hero*
BlindSpot #6. *Being a Hero or Savior*
BlindSpot #7. *Overwhelming Emotion*
BlindSpot #8. *Bad Timing*

Whatever you've checked, you're now better equipped for the hard work of change.

Handling Adversity

As you move ahead, realize that illuminating BlindSpots and dealing with them is an incremental process. Understand how hard it is to blow a whistle and say, "Stop! I'm not sure things are going right. I want to reassess this situation." It takes an act of courage to re-evaluate what you're doing. To help yourself handle any setbacks, try these techniques:

1. *Check and follow through on long- and short-term objectives.*

You need both long- and short-term goals to get what you want in life, but it's common to focus too much on one or the other. You may aim to become a top executive, yet bog down in unimportant local fights and office politics. These skirmishes sap energy and distract you from achieving the long-term objective: a promotion. It's akin to winning the battles and losing the war.

On the other hand, impatience can make you forget to set short-term goals in the first place—interim steps that get you where you ultimately want to go. For example, if the long-term goal is marriage, short-term objectives could include networking, joining organizations, or actively engaging in community affairs, all of which lead to meeting new people. You also might figure out how you come across and identify behaviors that turn others off.

2. *Ask, "How am I doing?"*

Along the way, mistakes, false starts, and periods of inertia will always happen. Expect and be alert to them. Don't beat yourself up if improvement is slow or you occasionally backslide. It's a great deal of work to figure out what's happening in your life.

Ask others for input on your progress, and pay attention to signs that you're becoming defensive about what you are hearing. Hotels, teachers, and parents all ask how they're doing, but many ignore the answer. The story of two restaurants illustrates what often occurs. In the first, an expensive new place, hot dishes arrive at the table cold and the waiter serves the wrong appetizer. At the end of the meal, the owner introduces himself and asks, "How was everything?" If you honestly tell him, you notice his eyes wandering around the room. He clearly can't wait to disengage. Then he issues a curt "Good night." Of course, you never return.

Another restaurant, successful for many years, stands out in bold contrast. On the few occasions when the service is slow, the owner sends over a complimentary drink or dessert. Once when rare sirloin arrived well done, he prepared a new steak and tore up the check. He not only serves good food, he acknowledges mistakes and deals with them. The message to patrons: "I care. I want to make you happy." There's a reason why such restaurants win loyal followings.

3. *Balance internal voices and external influences.*

Gut feelings are often a good starting point for decision making because without them, very few people would take risks or launch bold new ventures. On the other hand, intuition is not enough to carry you through. It's important to acknowledge signals in the pit of your stomach, but also necessary to hold them up to the light. Do they stand up when compared with the results of market research and outside feedback?

There may be times when you decide to go ahead regardless. Do so, however, only after taking responsibility for the decision. If the outcome is a disaster, bad luck had nothing to do with it. You decided on this risky plan. Ask yourself, too, "Can I afford to take the loss if this doesn't work out?"

Maybe you've stayed at a hotel in Florida many times. Over the years, you got to know the owner very well. When he tells you he plans to retire and sell the place, you immediately want to grab the opportunity. You love the location, amenities, and especially the golf course. You've recently sold your own business. However, you know the importance of due diligence. You take your time comparing the price and profitability of the hotel with other properties. You research financing, the local economy, and travel market forecasts In the end, the numbers don't add up. Reluctantly, you pass up the deal. You love the idea of owning the hotel and your own golf course, but you don't have the resources to risk absorbing a major loss. *Overwhelming Emotion* has hurt you in the past, but this time you've controlled your BlindSpot.

4. *Remember that you are not looking for perfection.*

The goal is to make you a little bit better at arriving at healthy decisions. *Looking for a Hero* is the biggest BlindSpot for one of our patients. This successful computer industry executive told us, "I attribute too much to people, and then I'm invariably disappointed. I'm also a sucker for personality. I have now learned to check out the reality with my wife. When she says, 'This is another case of hero worship,' I listen. I become too easily enamored of people, and I know that's a BlindSpot for me."

He recently put this insight to use when he heard a presentation by an investment advisor. "I liked him, and I was beginning to want to believe him. I wanted him to be telling the truth. Then I thought, 'Is he playing on my BlindSpot? There are some parts of his story that don't completely add up.' It was the first time I was able to recognize this relatively quickly. It's given me more confidence in my ability to make decisions about other people," he reports.

Coping with Others' BlindSpots

Life is difficult enough when you must handle your own BlindSpots. At times, you also have to deal with someone else's BlindSpots because they directly affect you. What do you do when another person tries to fix or change you? What's the best way to handle a family member who has mislabeled you or a professional savior who has made you a target? The first question in each case is: Does it bother you? The second question is: If you do mind, are you willing to address it?

Perhaps you were always the clumsy one in the family. That perception may have been triggered by a minor incident, or it may have been based on the person you were long ago. Maybe you were lazy in high school. Now you work very hard, but family members still see you as a sixteen-year-old slacker. If it bothers you and you want to be treated differently, try saying, "I think you have a BlindSpot about who I am and my accomplishments. Maybe I slept late when I was a teenager, but that was decades ago. You're relying on old information that no longer applies."

That kind of statement really grabs people's attention. Sometimes just identifying the BlindSpot and asking "What's going on here? I don't think you see me accurately," can change the person's perception—or at least his or her behavior toward you.

You can use a similar script when faced with a professional savior who has made you his next project. Here you can say, "I appreciate the generous impulse, but I don't want to (or need to) be rescued."

What if your parents want you to be a corporate attorney, but you have other plans? You can say something like, "You've got a BlindSpot about me. You want me to be a lawyer, but I don't have the necessary qualities. I don't even like the profession. I want to be a musician." When her family pushed her to become a doctor, one young woman took a course in chemistry and hated it. She told her father, "I hate science. Stop trying to make me an M.D. That's not what I want."

In situations where someone has power over you (such as a supervisor), your leverage is limited and a great deal of diplomacy may be required. Be aware that your ability to deal with the person's BlindSpot may be compromised and risks are involved. If you confront an obnoxious boss too directly, you may get a bad review or even get fired. You may decide that the job opportunity is worth putting up with him or her.

There are other times when you may have no choice but to live with another person's BlindSpot. You may say, "My boss loses his temper. There's no way I can get him to see how that turns me off. But I love the job, so I have to figure out how I'm going to tolerate this behavior or work around it."

Perhaps you're in a troubled marriage. Yet you decide, "Although this relationship isn't what I expected, it's far better than getting divorced." Some couples do look at the entire package—the family, the lifestyle, the friendships, and the social life—and decide that, on balance, it's worth staying. The temptation may be to get out, but leaving without seeing the negative consequences could itself be a BlindSpot.

You may feel that you don't want to bring up someone else's BlindSpot because it won't do any good. If the other person is unable to see it, you may have to figure out how to cope with the BlindSpot, just as you cope with anyone else's idiosyncrasies. Knowing the BlindSpot isn't yours can be very reassuring.

When You're Not Affected

On the other hand, sometimes another's BlindSpot does not directly impact on you—yet you care about the person and want to help. How often have you watched your friend, child, or spouse repeat a self-damaging mistake and mess up a relationship, career, or financial security? At one time or another you've probably been tempted to ask, "How can you be so blind? Don't you see that you're headed for trouble?" It's only human to want to help when someone important to you is about to get hurt. Unfortunately, however, there's not much you can do because people reject those who give unsolicited opinions.

Before you speak up, consider these factors:

What is the nature of the relationship? You can say to your grown child or someone else very close, "I'm concerned about what you're doing." But if you persist when the person isn't interested in hearing it, you violate boundaries. You do have to respect the limits set by another person. It's hard to sit passively by when you're thinking, "Disaster would be averted if only he or she could see things a bit more clearly." But sometimes you have to do just that.

What are the consequences of saying something (or nothing)? They depend on the nature of the person's behavior. If someone wants to keep marrying the wrong kind of person (in your opinion), that's his or her business—unless abuse is involved. If someone is suicidal, however, you have to pay attention. You may feel compelled to say, "You need to get help."

What is the risk to your relationship with the person? Weigh the consequences of the individual's reaction to your comments. Ask yourself, "What's the worst that will happen if I speak up?" Will the person get annoyed at you—or refuse to see you ever again? Some people are intensely private. A good way to protect the relationship is to ask, "Do you want my advice, or do you just want to vent?" When it's the latter, you must accept that.

Turn Failure Into Success and Move On

After making bad mistakes, patients commonly tell us, "At the time, it seemed like the right thing to do. I wish I could turn the clock back." Mistakes will happen. But when you're aware of your BlindSpots, you'll make wiser choices and have fewer missteps. You'll learn something from every misadventure, understanding what went wrong and what went right. The goal is to become smarter in the way you live your life and be able to say, "This is where I'm vulnerable and this is what I'm going to do to protect myself next time."

Once you see things more clearly, problems that seemed so knotty will begin to look less daunting. You will see more options and possibilities. What was so painful and mysterious will come sharply into focus and be easier to understand and manage. Gradually, recognizing and taking charge of your BlindSpots even becomes fun.

You've acquired the tools to do what you have to do. Start getting more of what you want right now. We wish you good luck.

About the Authors

Steven S. Simring, M.D., M.P.H. and Sue Klavans Simring, D.S.W. are coauthors of *Making Marriage Work for Dummies* and *The Compatibility Quotient.* They appear regularly on radio and have been guests on such national TV talk shows as *Montel Williams*, *Live with Regis and Kelly*, *Oprah*, *Maury Povich*, *Sally Jessy Raphael*, and *Ricki Lake.*

Dr. Steven Simring is coauthor of *The Race Trap* and *How to Win Back the One You Love.* He is on the faculty of the Columbia University College of Physicians and Surgeons and Director of the Columbia/Cornell Residency in Psychiatry and the Law, and the recipient of numerous awards for outstanding teaching. He has lectured extensively to both popular and professional audiences. Dr. Simring is a distinguished psychotherapist who has been retained as an expert psychiatrist in numerous highly publicized civil and criminal cases, and is a frequent guest on Court TV.

Dr. Sue Klavans Simring is a practicing psychotherapist who specializes in working with individuals and families. She is a lecturer at the Columbia University School of Social Work and is frequently called on by the media and professional organizations to discuss emotional and mental health issues.

Florence Isaacs is a freelance writer and author of six books: *Just A Note To Say . . . The Perfect Words for Every Occasion*; *Change Your Mind, Change Your Body* (with Ann Kerney Cooke, Ph.D.); *Business Notes*; *My Deepest Sympathies*; *Here's To You*; *Toxic Friends, True Friends.* She has contributed articles on health and medicine, relationships, communication, and etiquette to *Woman's Day*, *Good Housekeeping*,

Redbook, *Modern Bride*, *Fitness*, *Parents*, *Cosmopolitan*, *Parade*, *Reader's Digest*, and other leading publications. She is a past president of The American Society of Journalists and Authors.

Index